NATHANIEL HAWTHORNE

MILTON MELTZER

NATHANIEL HAWTHORNE

A BIOGRAPHY

Twenty-First Century Books
Minneapolis

Cover photo of Nathaniel Hawthorne used with permission from © Bettmann/CORBIS.

Photographs used with permission from © Bettmann/CORBIS, pp. 2, 68, 93, 99, 117; Peabody Essex Museum, Salem, MA, pp. 11, 17, 18, 21, 23, 24, 28, 33, 35, 39, 41, 47, 55, 83, 90, 113, 128 (all), 142; © North Wind Picture Archives, pp. 13, 57, 62, 69 right, 77, 78 right, 105, 119, 132 right; Library of Congress, pp. 16, 76 (LC-USZ62-13011), 78 left (LC-USZ62-10610), 98 right (LC-USZ62-93807), 107 (LC-DIG-cwpbh-02545), 138 (LC-USZ61-1938); Bowdoin College Museum of Art, Brunswick, Maine, Gift of Harold L. Berry, Class of 1901, p. 29; George J. Mitchell Dept. of Special Collections & Archives, Bowdoin College Library, Brunswick, Maine, pp. 31, 51; Bowdoin College Museum of Art, Brunswick, Maine, Bequest of Marian Bridge Maurice, p. 42; Concord Free Public Library, pp. 59, 67, 69 left, 86, 132 left; Massachusetts Historical Society, p. 63; Security Pacific Collection/Los Angeles Public Library, p. 81; National Park Service, Longfellow National Historic Site, p. 84; Boston Athenæum, gift of the estate of Mrs. James H. Beal, p. 87; Berkshire Athenaeum, Pittsfield, Massachusetts, p. 98 left; New Hampshire Historical Society, p. 111; The Bancroft Library, University of California, Berkeley, p. 116; Smithsonian American Art Museum, Washington, DC/Art Resource, NY, p. 122; Alinari/Art Resource, NY, p. 124; © CORBIS, p. 125; © Hulton Archive/Getty Images, p. 127; © Kevin Fleming/CORBIS, p. 143.

Copyright © 2007 by Milton Meltzer

Twenty-First Century Books
A division of Lerner Publishing Group
241 First Avenue North
Minneapolis, Minnesota 55401 U.S.A.

Website address: www.lernerbooks.com

Library of Congress Cataloging-in-Publication Data

Meltzer, Milton, 1915–
Nathaniel Hawthorne : a biography / by Milton Meltzer.
p. cm. — (American literary greats)
Includes bibliographical references and index.
ISBN-13: 978-0-7613-3459-0 (lib. bdg. : alk. paper)
ISBN-10: 0-7613-3459-9 (lib. bdg. : alk. paper)
1. Hawthorne, Nathaniel, 1804–1864. 2. Novelists, American—
19th century—Biography. I. Title. II. Series.
PS1881.M43 2007   813'.3—dc22   2005000018

Manufactured in the United States of America
1 2 3 4 5 6 – BP – 12 11 10 09 08 07

Also by Milton Meltzer

Contents

Introduction

Once in a while, over the long span of recorded history, there is an explosion of talent. Men and women, seeming to come from nowhere, create great works—in the arts, the sciences, philosophy. It happened in Greece in the fifth century B.C., and in the Italian city of Florence in the Renaissance of the fifteenth century, to give but two examples.

It has happened in our country too. Take that brief period of the early 1850s. New and very different voices were heard in literature. Several writers broke old molds to create original works. There were Emerson, Thoreau, Whitman, Poe, Dickinson, Melville, and Hawthorne. All wrote their best work in those few years. Truly it was an American Renaissance.

It is Nathaniel Hawthorne's story that this book deals with. You may know him for his two greatest novels—*The Scarlet Letter* (1850) and *The House of the Seven Gables* (1851). He also wrote many highly valued short stories, and children's books too.

His was not an easy life. Few American writers coasted into fame and fortune in that time. The story starts long before his birth—when his Puritan ancestors, the Hathornes*, persecuted Quakers and others accused of witchcraft.

---

* Hawthorne's family spelled the name "Hathorne" in the generations before him. Nathaniel inserted the *w* after his college years. To avoid confusion, the form Hawthorne is used throughout this book.

A Tormented Heart

SALEM, THE MASSACHUSETTS TOWN where Nathaniel Hawthorne was born on July 4, 1804, was one of the earliest American settlements of the English Puritans in the 1600s. The first immigrant of the Hawthorne line was William Hawthorne. Settling in Salem in 1630, he became one of the leading men of the colony who laid its foundation as a theocratic society. He held many offices, including magistrate, and as a major fought in the battles to force the Indians out of their homelands.

For those early Puritan settlers, purity meant ridding the community of anyone whose political or religious beliefs differed from theirs. William Hawthorne was famed for his pitiless severity toward the Quakers, purging them by force and violence.

His son, Judge John Hawthorne, rigid as the father, rose to power when New England was ridding itself of witches by hanging and burning them. In 1692 charges of witchcraft shook the village of Salem. The chief questioner of the accused was Judge Hawthorne. He always acted as though he assumed them guilty,

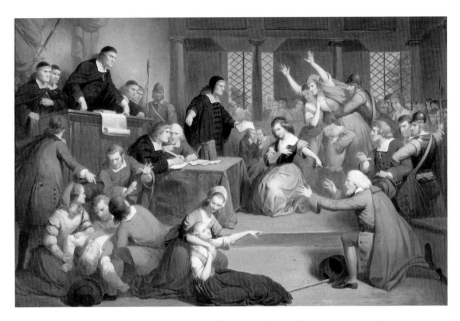

The Salem trials resulted in the last witchcraft executions in American history. Nineteen people, both men and women, were convicted and hanged as witches. This 1855 painting of the trial of George Jacobs Sr. (kneeling, front right) *captures the atmosphere of hysteria that pervaded the proceedings.*

and he earned lasting notoriety for his harsh sentencing of innocent people convicted on false evidence.

While the witch-hunt craze lasted, men and women, young and old, were jailed, their property confiscated, and they were forced to invent testimony against innocent others. The court's central aim was to get a confession out of the accused. About fifty people gave in to the intense pressure, and some were executed.

The Puritan dissenters from the Church of England had sailed across the Atlantic to found a new Eden in America. But like other people, some of them sinned. The Puritan community was not free of thieves, murderers, and adulterers. And when they were caught, they were severely punished. The stocks and the pillory were rarely empty. Judge John Hawthorne had no trouble ordering punishment: Cut off this guilty man's ear, burn that women's tongue with red-hot iron, split that offender's nose. He had women stripped and whipped through the town at the tail of a cart. Some were forced to wear on the breast of their clothing a scarlet letter, the sign of sin. This Hawthorne earned the reputation of chasing down the wicked like a bloodhound.

The Quakers especially were denounced by the Puritans as a fanatical sect bringing vapors from hell. Unlike the Puritans, Quakers did not believe that you needed a salaried ministry to cultivate the Inner Light and be saved. Their radical sect was founded by George Fox (1624–1691), an English cobbler. He believed that the Divine spirit could speak directly to us. He formed the Society of Friends, called Quakers. They stood firmly against all warfare, whether religious or worldly, and often suffered beatings and brandings and prison terms for their beliefs.

Women were prominent early in their movement. If God was in everyone, then women as well as men could be chosen by the Inner Light to be ministers. Salem's Quakers were fined again and again if they did not attend the established church, and some were banished from the colony. Four Quakers were hanged in Boston. When Charles II (1630–1685) came to the English throne, he ordered that no more Quakers should be executed. But that did not stop the Puritans from sentencing them to other brutal punishments short of death.

Nathaniel Hawthorne, with his dramatic skill, captures the dreadful experience of Ann Coleman, a Quaker victim of William Hawthorne's judgment:

> Naked from the waist upward, and bound to the tail of a cart, [she] is dragged through the Main-street at the pace of a brisk walk, while the constable follows with a whip of knotted cords. A strong-armed fellow is that constable; and

Mary Dyer, a Quaker woman, is pictured here being led to her execution in Massachusetts in the 1600s. Quakers suffered torture, imprisonment, banishment, and in the case of a few, execution for their religious beliefs.

each time that he flourishes his lash in the air, you see a frown wrinkling and twisting his brow, and, at the same instant, a smile upon his lips. He loves his business, faithful officer that he is, and puts his soul into every stroke, zealous to fulfill the injunction of Major Hawthorne's warrant, in the spirit and to the letter. There came down a stroke that has drawn blood! Ten such stripes are to be given in Salem, ten in Boston, and ten in Dedham; and, with those thirty stripes of blood upon her, she is to be driven into the forest. . . . Heaven grant, that, as the rain of so many years has wept upon it, time after time, and washed it all away, so there may have been a dew of mercy, to cleanse this cruel blood-stain out of the record of the persecutor's life!

It was a family bloodstain Nathaniel Hawthorne could never rid himself of, even after more than a hundred years had passed since those ancestors died. Later generations of Hawthornes failed to gain high position. They became almost a forgotten family, except in Nathaniel's mind. He himself seemed to believe the legend that a curse had been flung upon the Hawthornes by a witch on the scaffold about to be hanged.

There is no evidence of William or John Hawthorne ever suffering pangs of conscience. But Nathaniel bore their guilt, and his tormented heart would influence what he chose to write about, and how he did it.

The World of Salem

THE YEAR Nathaniel Hawthorne was born, 1804, was the year Thomas Jefferson was reelected president of the United States. And the same year that Lewis and Clark set out on the expedition that began the exploration of the American West. In 1804 about six million people lived in the young republic, the same number that now live in just one state, Massachusetts.

Salem, Nathaniel's birthplace, was where he would set many of his stories. Ships from this port on the New England coast sailed round the world. The protected harbor encouraged trade and in the early 1700s, shipbuilding and allied industries were booming. From its wharves, ships carried away fish and other supplies and brought back the exotic treasures of the Indies and China. Yankee captains drove profitable bargains wherever they sailed, piling up great wealth. Many made fortunes so quickly they retired by the age of thirty.

Along with the city's swift commercial development came cultural expansion. Yankee Salem now knew something of Oriental

In 1804 Nathaniel Hawthorne was born in this two-story wood house that was located at 27 Union Street in Salem, Massachusetts. Nathaniel's father was also born in this house in 1776.

luxury, and superb new mansions in the Federal style were built during the great maritime period.

Nathaniel was the son of a sea captain, Nathaniel Hawthorne, and of Elizabeth Clarke Manning Hawthorne. The child would grow up without a father. For while on one of the long voyages that often took him away from home, Captain Hawthorne, at thirty-two, died of yellow fever in Dutch Guiana, on the coast of South America. Nathaniel, only four, would never stop mourning his missing parent.

The Hawthornes who came after their notorious seventeenth-century ancestors are only dim figures in the past—earning a living on the sea or by farming. Nathaniel's parents married in 1801. Besides their son, they had two daughters: Elizabeth, born in 1802, and Mary Louisa, in 1808.

We know little about the ancestry of Nathaniel's mother. The Mannings came from England in 1679 and took up business enterprises. Nathaniel's uncle, Robert Manning, launched a successful stagecoach line between towns around Boston. His experiments also earned him a reputation as an authority on the cultivation of fruit trees.

Nathaniel inherited certain characteristics from both of his parents. People who had known Nathaniel's father spoke of him as a silent, reserved, severe man. Nathaniel was said to have inherited from him a certain sternness, a moodiness, a tendency

Nathaniel's father followed in the maritime tradition of many of his ancestors. Captain Hawthorne was abroad during his son's birth and early childhood, and he died on one of his trips abroad when Nathaniel was only four years old.

to solitude. And from his mother, her gray eyes, gentle manners, reserve, and thoughtfulness. As for religion, the Hawthorne tribe, once fanatical Puritans, had now become Unitarians.

Although Salem prospered in the maritime trade, not every one of its seafarers piled up wealth. Your ship could be wrecked in storms, pirates could plunder your cargo, and disease could wipe out your crew. The Hawthornes were not among the luckier ones. They lived in modest frame houses on congested narrow streets. The more prosperous captains and merchants enjoyed grand homes and sent their sons to Harvard College.

Nathaniel would make his home in Salem for some thirty years, off and on. Sometimes he said he loved the town. Other

Hawthorne claimed to despise his childhood home of Salem, Massachusetts, and yet he was drawn to make his home there for most of his adult life. Perhaps it was hard to resist the idyllic beauty of the seaside town as shown in this painting by Alvin Fisher of the 1800s.

times, he hated it. In his writings he often ignored the aristocratic side of life. He was not welcomed into the homes of the upper class. He liked to wander the streets, observing the carts of the butchers, the fishmongers, the vegetable peddlers, the bakers, the scissors-grinders, all crying their wares, making such noises "as ever did petty violence to human ears."

In his notebooks, where he recorded his more private thoughts and feelings, it's evident that Nathaniel liked to escape stuffy middle-class life to visit the neighborhoods and hangouts of the "lower social orders." He enjoyed watching the seamen flirting with young girls, and "half-stewed fellows" brawling in the streets, calling the "shoutings and hallooings, laughter-oaths-generally a good-natured tumult."

Yet, in a letter to his bride-to-be, Sophia Peabody, he asked if she didn't think that Salem was "really the most hateful place in all the world?" (At that time neither had seen much of any other place.) He wondered how he could "write all my tales in this same region of sleepyhead and stupidity."

In what way and to what degree did the world of Salem determine Hawthorne's art? All writers, perhaps Hawthorne especially, are too complicated for easy answers. Creation is mysterious. But what we do know, says the scholar Margaret B. Moore, is that "many of Hawthorne's best legends sprang from the town that he so loved and hated, for the Salem world of the past was essential to his literary imagination."

3
A Right and a Wrong

CAPTAIN HAWTHORNE left little money when he died. His widow had to move with her three children from their small home on Union Street to the tall gray house of her parents, the Mannings, on Herbert Street, one block away. It was chock-full of family—four uncles and four aunts, all unmarried, with Grandfather Richard Manning presiding. He owned large tracts of land in Maine and was the founder of the profitable Salem and Boston Stage Company. A kindly man, uneducated himself, he had seen to it that his sons were schooled. One of them, Robert Manning, was the brother Nathaniel's mother looked to for guidance. He took charge of her children's education.

The only person in that large family who remained distant was Nathaniel's mother. It was said that Mrs. Hawthorne rarely left her room. She ate her meals alone and relied on a servant to look after her children. Although still in her twenties, she continued to be the grieving widow who would not permit herself any pleasures. To young Nathaniel, she must have been a wraithlike mother who could offer only a faint smile in passing, and none of the hugging and kissing her child needed and missed terribly.

In that time, death at an early age was almost taken for granted. Salem lost many young men at sea, and disease, accident, and suicide made death commonplace. With his father gone and his mother emotionally distant, Nathaniel had his two sisters to lean on: Elizabeth (1802–1887), called Ebe, two years older, beautiful, and in temperament much like her brother. And Maria Louisa (1808–1852), called Louisa, four years younger, who never saw her father. She grew up to be a gentle, witty woman.

As a substitute father, Robert Manning tried to set guidelines for Nathaniel. It must have been a difficult task, for later, Hawthorne had little to say about Uncle Robert or the other Mannings. Children orphaned by the loss of a father would figure in some of his stories. Perhaps in his imagination he conjured up

Nathaniel's uncle Robert Manning helped care for Nathaniel and his two sisters when the Hawthornes moved into their grandparents' house after their father's death.

an idealized father that no substitute father, dealing with the day-to-day emotional realities of a growing child, could compete with.

Later, Hawthorne's older sister, Elizabeth, said that Nathaniel was "the especial pet of all" in the Manning household, "particularly petted" because "his health was then delicate and he had frequent illnesses."

But no one thought of the child as a budding genius. Soon after his father died, four-year-old Nathaniel was sent to one of Salem's private schools. There he learned his ABCs and began to read. When he turned six, he took lessons for two years at another private school. It was said that by now he was reading John Bunyan's *Pilgrim's Progress* and Edmund Spenser's *The Faerie Queene*. Both books were allegories. That is, the characters did not depict real people but rather stood for something that was symbolic. That way of viewing the world—or veiling it!—became second nature to Hawthorne.

Like many children, he believed he could have more fun out of school than in. The Manning family's stagecoach drivers used to hoist the boy up on their front seat and spin along the high road with Nathaniel enjoying the sights of the countryside.

When he was seven, while playing in the schoolyard one day, he hurt his foot, and he had to be carried home. All sorts of remedies were tried. Nothing worked. At one time, he seemed to be better, but then some other illness took hold, and he couldn't move his limbs at all for a while. For about fifteen months, at a time when youngsters grow fast and enjoy the pleasures of physical action, he lived a limited life, limping or needing crutches, lying down a lot, reading to pass the time, daydreaming . . .

Still, his schooling continued. At the time of the injury, he had been studying with Joseph E. Worcester, a Yale graduate. While Nathaniel was laid up, the teacher came to his home to help with the lessons. Many years later, Worcester would become famous for compiling his great *Dictionary of the English Language,* briefly the major American dictionary, until a new edition of Webster's *American Dictionary* appeared in 1864.

Those few years were a time of great national excitement, and of personal loss for Nathaniel. The War of 1812 changed Salem. Nathaniel's uncles speculated in ships and in guns. The famous battle between the American warship *Chesapeake,* and the British *Shannon,* was fought offshore Salem, with Nathaniel among the crowds who watched it. Both his grandfather Manning and his grandmother Hawthorne died soon after.

In 1816 the Hawthornes spend a summer in Maine, at Raymond, where the Mannings owned land near Sebago Lake, at

When he was twelve years old, Hawthorne spent a summer at the Mannings' residence in Raymond, Maine.

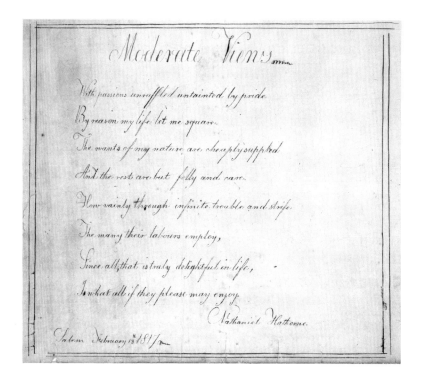

When Hawthorne was just fourteen years old, he exhibited great maturity in a poem entitled Moderate Views. *He wrote, "The wants of my nature are cheaply supplied, / And the rest are but folly and care."*

the edge of what was then wilderness. (Maine was still a territory. It would not enter the Union as a state until 1820.) It was a deliciously free time for Nathaniel—no school, a wildness to explore, and lots of time for reading. Sir Walter Scott's novels and Shakespeare's plays were among his favorites.

Back in Salem, Nathaniel's education expanded to dancing school. He learned how to do the minuet, the hornpipe, and the jig. No longer lame, a report held that he "could stand and leap as high as his shoulder." His dancing teacher, a Frenchman, advertised that "the object in teaching young people to dance

does not consist wholly in the amusement which it yields them,
but is intended to give a polish to their manners and grace to their carriage and movements."

In 1818 the Mannings built a home for Mrs. Hawthorne in Maine, right next to Uncle Richard's. Later Nathaniel would write that this brief time with his mother and sisters was the happiest period of his life. It ended in the spring of 1819, when Uncle Robert ordered him back to Salem to get on with his schooling.

This time it was at the school of Samuel Archer, a Dartmouth graduate. He was a devoted teacher. Long after, upon his death, the Salem newspaper said his moral influence upon the boys in the twenty years of his teaching was "truly wonderful. . . . He convinced all under his care that to every act and thought there was a right and a wrong, and that their own self-respect, their safety and happiness, as well as the favor of God, could only be promoted and secured by choosing the right."

Archer offered a wide range of studies—in grammar and composition, geography, chemistry, astronomy, bookkeeping, philosophy, mathematics, and Latin and Greek. The classes ran from 8:30 A.M. to 4:30 P.M., with a half-hour break at midday.

Family letters between Nathaniel and his mother and older sister Ebe, living in Maine, indicate that Nathaniel was not eager to go on with his schooling. He even used as an excuse that his mother could hardly spare him. He wished he was back in the Maine woods, said one aunt, "yet he seems to be convinced of the necessity of preparing to do something."

College Years

BUT WHAT EXACTLY was Nathaniel to do? Uncle Robert thought maybe becoming a merchant would be the right thing. Not Mr. Archer! He believed Nathaniel was talented and should go to college. This probably surprised the Mannings, for none of them were college graduates.

It was under Archer that Nathaniel tried his hand at poetry. He wrote his family in Maine that he was "full of scraps of poetry." One such "scrap" ran:

> Lady fair, will you not listen
> To my ardent vows of love?
> Love that in my eyes doth glisten,
> And is firm as Heaven above.

Early in 1820, young Hawthorne began to prepare for college entrance under the private tutoring of a Salem lawyer, Benjamin L. Oliver Jr. He came to Oliver every day at seven in the morning to

recite his lessons. For entertainment he went to a concert in Salem
and saw *King Lear* in Boston, and that summer he learned to swim.
To his mother he wrote, "I am 16 years old. In five years I shall
belong to myself." (Almost two years had passed since he had last
seen her.) "You are in great danger of having one learned man in
your family," he warned her. But in what direction should his
higher education go? His letter continues:

> The being a Minister is of course out of the Question. I
> should not think that even you would desire me to choose
> so dull a way of life. . . . As to Lawyers there are so many of
> them already that one-half of them (upon a moderate cal-
> culation) are in a state of actual starvation. A Physician
> then seems to be "Hobson's Choice," but yet I should not
> like to live by the diseases and infirmities of my fellow
> Creatures. . . . Oh that I was rich enough to live without a
> profession. What do you think of my becoming an Author,
> and relying for support upon my pen. Indeed I think the
> illegibility of my handwriting is very authorlike. How
> proud you would feel to see my works praised by the
> reviewers. . . . But Authors are always poor devils, and
> therefore Satan may take them. . . .

He was reaching out more widely in his reading, bragging to a
sister that he hadread almost all the books published the last hundred years. Out of his skimpy earnings he managed to buy a book
or two. With his sister Louisa's help he published (hand-lettered) a
few issues of a satiric newspaper called the *Spectator*. It was a take-
off on the local papers, with essays, poems, and news items. Even
this early, he showed a mastery of style.

Bowdoin College in Brunswick, Maine, was the family's choice
for Hawthorne. It was fairly new, and not too far from Raymond
where his mother was, so he could see her on weekends. It was not

POETRY.

For the Spectator.

ADDRESS TO THE SUN.

Glorious harbinger of day,
When the Moon her course has run,
When all darkness fleets away,
Then we see thee, glorious Sun.

MARIA LOUISA HATHORNE.

For the Spectator.

ADDRESS TO THE MOON.

How sweet the silver Moon's pale ray,
Falls trembling on the distant bay,
O'er which the breezes sigh no more,
Nor billows lash the sounding shore.
Say, do the eyes of those I love,
Behold thee as thou soar'st above,
Lonely, majestick and serene,
The calm and placid evening's Queen?
Say, if upon thy peaceful breast,
Departed spirits find their rest,
For who would wish a fairer home,
Than in that bright, refulgent dome?

No. 5. N. HATHORNE

THE SPECTATOR.

EDITED BY N. HATHORNE.

MONDAY, SEPT. 18, 1820.

ON HOPE.

Hope is a feeling which is inherent in the human breast, from which it can never be totally banished. It was wisely bestowed upon us by the Author of all Good, as a support through the troubles and afflictions which beset us in this world. In the darkest days of distress Hope never deserts us, but bids us look forward with confidence to scenes of happiness. Without its cheering influence man would sink into despair. Without its support the bed of death is a scene of unspeakable terror and dismay.

With the hope of a glorious immortality, it may truly and emphatically be said that "Dying is but going Home."

Our Readers will pardon the many faults and inaccuracies which they find in the Spectator, when they consider the different offices we have to perform. In the first place, we study Latin and Greek. Secondly we write in the employ of Wm. Manning Esq. Thirdly, we are Secretary, Treasurer, and Manager of the Pin Society. Fourthly we are Editor of the Spectator. Fifthly, sixthly and lastly our own Printers, Printing Press and Types.

This handwritten fifth issue of the Spectator *was published by Hawthorne on September 18, 1820.*

rated as highly as Harvard or Yale, but was less expensive. In 1821 eight professors made up the faculty, and 108 young men, 38 of them freshmen, the student body. He passed the entrance exams, given orally by the faculty. He lived in a student dormitory and took his meals in the home of a young professor.

The college year was divided into three semesters, with tuition $24 for each, room rent $10, and meals about $2 a week. The courses required were Greek, Latin, mathematics (including astronomy, surveying, and navigation), and philosophy. The science curriculum offered natural history, geography, and chemistry. From today's standpoint, there was too little attention to history, modern languages, and modern literature.

All students had to attend religious services every morning and to take part in weekly orations. These two obligations

Hawthorne skipped as often as he could, although it cost him small fines.

At Bowdoin he met students with whom he would remain close all his life. First of all, there was Horatio Bridge. Hawthorne believed he was his best friend in all the world. Bridge would build a notable career in government service. Of great importance too in Hawthorne's future was Franklin Pierce. He would devote himself to politics and ride that career into the White House. Then there was Henry Wadsworth Longfellow, who would become America's most popular poet. Still another classmate was Calvin Stowe, later a minister, reformer, and the husband of Harriet Beecher Stowe, author of *Uncle Tom's Cabin*. Hawthorne joined a college literary society, the Athenaean. He described it as

Hawthorne was one of several well-known men who were in residence at Bowdoin College in the early 1820s. Fellow students included future president Franklin Pierce and poet Henry Wadsworth Longfellow.

progressive or democratic. When Andrew Jackson, the Democratic candidate for president, campaigned in 1824, the members were avid supporters.

Fellow students have left us glimpses of what Hawthorne was like in those years. He was described as a slender lad, having a massive head, with dark, brilliant, and most expressive eyes, heavy eyebrows, and a profusion of dark hair. When full grown, he was over five feet, ten inches tall. Bridge described him of having a habit of carrying his head a little to one side, but with a square and firm walk. And Bridge described Hawthone's voice as having deep musical tones.

In college Hawthorne was not the morbid, withdrawn creature as many later came to regard him. Bridge remembered him as having a much more fun-loving disposition than indicated in his writings. He liked to gamble at cards, with a quart of wine going to the winner. He drank at the taverns, smoked, and cut classes. Students were sometimes suspended or even expelled for gambling or drinking, but he escaped with only fifty-cent fines. In his junior year, fines cost him nearly six dollars.

There are no reports of any affairs with girls in the town, though Hawthorne apparently displayed an appreciation of the opposite sex. (At any rate, he would not marry until he was thirty-eight.) Years later, Hawthorne recalled some of the pleasures of his college years: gathering blueberries under the pine trees, watching the great fogs tumbling down the Androscoggin River, shooting pigeons and gray squirrels in the woods, and fishing for trout.

In 1822 his mother left Maine to move back to Salem. Unable to pay the expense of traveling that far on vacations, Nathaniel was invited by classmates to their nearby homes. His letters to family moan about shortage of funds or brag about an oration he gave in chapel before a crowded audience. He missed the grand occasion when Uncle Robert married and joked that it was too bad, for he needed to learn how to behave when it was his turn for marriage.

Hawthorne's silhouette, one of a series made of the Bowdoin graduating class of 1825

His letters say little about his studies, nor do they speculate about the future. But in 1825, not long before graduation, he wrote his sister Elizabeth that he was making progress on his novel, (probably *Fanshawe*) and let her see some stories he had written. He worried that the Mannings might expect too much of their college man. For, he said, "I have thought much about the subject and have finally come to the conclusion that I shall never make a distinguished figure in the world and all I hope or wish is to plod along with the multitude."

Maybe he was judging himself by his college rating, for he graduated in the fall of 1825 eighteenth in a class of thirty-nine. At commencement, Longfellow, fourth in their class, gave a speech on American literature. In the end, however, it was Hawthorne, not Longfellow, who would make the deeper mark in that field.

The Mystery of Sin

THE AUTHOR'S CAREER Hawthorne had joked about in his college letters became his single concern when he returned to Salem in 1825 to live in his mother's home. To write well, you must read a lot. That was a common belief (that still holds true). In the next ten years he would borrow 1,200 books from the circulating library of the Salem Athenaeum. He read books of all sorts. Among them were novels he studied for their artistry. He particularly enjoyed life stories, or biographies. He studied early American history, digging into original sources when possible. What happened in those colonial times? Why did people act the way they did? What did it reveal of human character? How did those men and women see themselves?

Mornings he devoted to writing. In the afternoon when the weather was good he took long walks, sometimes to Gallows Hill, where the witches had been hanged. His evenings were spent in reading. You recall that while at college he had begun work on a novel called *Fanshawe*. He must have gone on with it in Salem. We

Hawthorne occasionally visited Gallows Hill in Salem, the infamous site where nineteen men and women accused of witchcraft were hanged in 1692. The town's legacy and his family members' participation in the trials would influence some of Hawthorne's later writings.

know little about it, for it would get published only at his own expense—$100. And without his name attached. He was so disappointed by the experience that he had all the copies he could get hold of destroyed and never mentioned the book again.

When short of money, he did clerical chores for the Manning stagecoach firm or edited some of Uncle Robert's articles on fruit cultivation to be published in the *New England Farmer*. He claimed to have worked hard to shape the words into pretty sentences.

While fiddling with *Fanshawe*, Hawthorne discovered he could do much better with short pieces. These were sketches of local life, historical tales, and allegories. Some of these he called "twice-told tales," because he had heard or read them first and then had transformed them through his own vivid imagination.

"No other American writer," said the literary historian Van Wyck Brooks in the 1930s, "had revealed such a gift for finding his proper subjects; no other had so consciously pursued his ends." Writing—it isn't easy. You do it by yourself. It involves hard work, lots of rewriting, tossing out stuff that looks awful, starting over again, sweating over the right form, the right word, the right tone, the right meaning. Then, if you think you have done your best, getting it published is next. That's quite another thing. For it means finding a publisher who will invest in editing, printing, distributing, and promoting what you've written, whether in a magazine or as a book.

After saluting Edgar Allan Poe as "a craftsman of exquisite skill," Van Wyck Brooks said that Hawthorne was "his only rival in the 1830s in the art of prose composition and the writing of tales." The recognition was terribly slow in coming. The first stories Hawthorne wrote after college were turned down by a number of publishers. Sick to his stomach as they piled upon his desk, he threw several of the manuscripts into the fire.

He worked alone, in his tiny room at the top of the house. But when the chance to plunge into exciting public events occurred, he rushed out to be part of it. His sister Elizabeth said that military drills, political rallies, firemen's musters always drew him. Hearing the fire bells tolling, he raced to the burning buildings.

Away from home, his shyness faded. He was freer more often with people on the wrong side of the tracks than with the genteel folk of his own class. The upper crust detested Andrew Jackson, the Democratic president, but to Hawthorne he was "the greatest man we ever had." After his reelection in 1832, the president visited Salem, and Hawthorne walked out to the edge of town not to meet him or speak to him, but "only look at him."

The summer season, Hawthorne soon learned, was not a good time for him to write. His creative drive slackened, and he quit his desk. He took many trips, mostly fairly short ones, either

*After graduating from Bowdoin in 1825, Hawthorne
returned to live in his family's house on Herbert Street. He
would later call the home Castle Dismal. The window to
his room is on the fourth floor.*

with family members or alone. On these journeys, he packed his
notebooks with detailed observations of characters and incidents
that might prove usable when back at his desk.

He delighted in encounters with oddball characters, people of
questionable habits, who he met at the local taverns where he
would hang out, drinking, like everyone else. As a handsome

young man, looking somehow different, people would come up to ask him who he was and where he was from.

"I make innumerable acquaintances," he told Louisa, "and sit down, on the doorsteps in the midst of squires, judges, generals, and all the potentates of the land, discussing about the Salem Murder, the cowskinning of Isaac Hill, the price of hay, and the value of horseflesh." Jottings in his letters and notebooks often found their way into his stories.

Except for *Fanshawe* and one piece in the *Salem Gazette*, it was five years before Hawthorne was published. And then for another eleven years, his name never appeared as author of his stories. This was by his own choosing; he preferred to be anonymous. "For a good many years," he wrote a friend long after, "I was the obscurest man of letters in America." He wondered whether he was wasting his own and the world's time.

Somehow, in 1829, a Boston publisher named Goodrich ran across a stray copy of *Fanshawe* and liked it enough to find out who the author was. He got Hawthorne to submit several stories for *The Token*, a book Goodrich issued annually that people used for gifts. Some of Hawthorne's best work appeared in it, always unsigned. Payment, never certain, came to less than a dollar per printed page.

In one of his early stories, "The Devil in Manuscript," a fictional author tosses his rejected manuscripts into a blazing fire, moaning that "no American publisher will meddle with an American work, seldom if by a known writer, and never if by a new one, unless at the writer's risk."

This was a period in the nineteenth century when there was no international copyright law to protect an author's work. American publishers made easy money by stealing the work of popular British writers, paying them not one penny in royalties. Why sign a contract with an unknown young writer like Hawthorne when you could publish Charles Dickens for

nothing? (Not until 1896 was an international copyright conven-
tion adopted that protected the rights of all writers.)

Readers of Hawthorne's work—from his early short stories through his novels—find a theme to be the loss of innocence. Characters undergo experiences that open up knowledge of themselves and of others. They learn what makes the world go round. They begin to grasp the complexity of human nature. And what they come to understand changes their lives forever. More than once, his narratives carry young characters through an experience that reveals to them the existence of sin in the world.

"Often enough," writes his biographer James R. Mellow, "with Hawthorne's sinners the deed is only hinted at. The crime may occur in some penumbral past, but the conscience will be explored with the skill of a surgeon probing diseased flesh. The mystery of sin is what absorbs him."

A Captive in a Dungeon

HOW MUCH OF HIS WRITING Hawthorne destroyed is impossible to tell at this distance. But between 1830 and 1834, a few of his tales did reach print. Then in 1835, seventeen more were published, five more the next year, and in 1837 and 1938, another thirteen.

A lot of hard work for very little pay. From *The Token* he got only $108 for the eight pieces they published in 1837. The *New England Magazine* gave him only $140 for fourteen pieces. Unable to support himself on such a meager income, Hawthorne in 1836 took a job as editor of Goodrich's *American Magazine of Useful and Entertaining Knowledge*. The salary was $500 a year. His task was to fill the pages of the monthly magazine with all sorts of "service" pieces—advice on how to be a success, how to choose a husband or a wife, how to get an education, live well, be nice to people, and stay moral.

The job meant he had to leave Salem for Boston, where he found a room in a boardinghouse. He needed to draw on a great

In this 1835 portrait of Hawthorne, artist Henry Inman captured the look of a man who has experienced disappointment in his life.

variety of reference books for material. Denied the use of the Boston Athenaeum's library, he induced sister Elizabeth to borrow books from Salem's Athenaeum and to whip up pieces he would then edit.

He didn't pretend he was doing anything distinguished. He was openly cynical about it with his sister. He claimed to be able toss off a biography or a history in no time. All he had to do was take any old magazine article and squeeze it into the space he needed to fill. He advised her, however, not to look for anything really good!

Goodrich made lovely promises but rarely kept them. Hawthorne put out two issues of the magazine before he was paid—and then only half what was due him. Yet he accepted the publisher's offer to concoct a two-volume work called *Peter Parley's Universal History on the Basis of Geography*. It would be what the trade called a scissors-and-paste job. (Nevertheless, the work was still selling twenty years later; many schools adopted it for classroom use.) He was paid $100, which he handed over to Elizabeth for her indispensable help.

Then, in August 1836, after some eight months on Goodrich's payroll, he quit the job. Perhaps because he could no longer stand the hackwork, or because he wasn't being paid enough to live decently. It was back to Salem to hole up again in his attic room. Eleven years had passed since Bowdoin. What had he done to achieve fame and fortune? Little that anyone knew of or was willing to pay decently for. Yet others had made it in the literary world. Take Longfellow and Whittier—readers and critics knew who they were. But who knew the name Nathaniel Hawthorne?

It was lucky for Hawthorne that he had his faithful college friend Bridge in whom to confide his inmost feelings. He wrote Bridge that he felt like he was helplessly adrift. Bridge, sensitive and caring, would write again and again, trying to restore his friend's faith in his talents and his future. He would assure Hawthorne that he just had another case of the blues, and admonish him not to give up to them.

Without letting Hawthorne know, Bridge wrote to Goodrich, offering to guarantee $250 against any loss if Goodrich would publish a collection to be called *Twice-Told Tales*.

For *Twice-Told Tales*, Hawthorne selected eighteen of his previously published pieces, aiming to please the broadest audience. Several light sketches went in, those with happy endings. Only two dealt with the dark side of early Puritan days. From some of

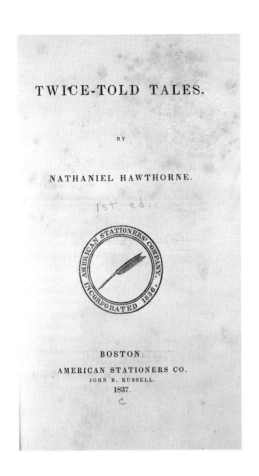

Several of Hawthorne's most popular short stories were reprinted under the title Twice-Told Tales, *so named because they had been previously published in magazines.*

the stories he deleted lines that might upset his more genteel readers. His strongest stories—those later considered among his early masterworks—he left out.

Excited as he was about the immediate prospect of publication, Hawthorne still showed signs of depression. You must snap out of it, Bridge wrote. Chiding him for never having confidence enough in himself, he assured him that someday he would be famous. Even after the book was launched in March 1837, Hawthorne still sounded blue, and Bridge suggested that maybe their college classmate Franklin Pierce, now a leader of Jacksonian Democrats in Congress, might help get him a government job.

Hawthorne met Horatio Bridge (left) *while at Bowdoin College. The two remained friends, with Bridge offering not only financial help but also emotional support to the author.*

In those days a writer with a good reputation stood a fair chance of winning such an appointment.

During that summer of 1837, Hawthorne spent nearly two months in Augusta, Maine, living with Bridge, who was supervising the building of a dam across the Kennebec River. It strengthened the close bond between them, with Hawthorne coming to admire Bridge all the more for his "excellent temper and warm heart, never varying from a code of honor and principle."

During that summer, Hawthorne heard from Longfellow, recently appointed a professor of foreign languages at Harvard. Hawthorne had sent him a copy of *Twice-Told Tales*, and the poet had responded warmly. Now Hawthorne told him:

> By some witchcraft or other . . . I have been carried apart
> from the main current of life, and find it impossible to get

Panic of 1837

In 1837 Hawthorne noted that hard times were surely limiting the sales of his work as well as those of other authors. This was the Panic of 1837, the first of the great depressions in American history. Many people had been gambling with investments and business had grown increasingly shaky. Crop failures in the spring hastened the economic collapse. Banks and factories closed. Mechanics and laborers suffered badly. Prices of food and fuel shot up, and desperate people rioted in the streets.

back again . . . I have secluded myself from society and yet I never meant any such thing, nor dreamed what sort of life I was going to lead. I have made a captive of myself and put me into a dungeon; and now I cannot find the key to let myself out—and if the door were open I should be almost afraid to come out. . . . For the last ten years I have not lived, but only dreamed about living. . . . As to my literary efforts, I do not think much of them—neither is it worthwhile to be ashamed of them. They would have been better, I trust, if written under more favorable circumstances. . . . I have seen so little of the world, that I have nothing but thin air to concoct my stories of, and it is not easy to give a lifelike semblance to such shadowy stuff. . . .

Longfellow praised *Twice-Told Tales* in one of the leading journals, the *North American Review* (July 1837). He called the book a "delightful" treatment of themes from colonial New England times, and commended the author for "the exceeding beauty of his bright, poetic style."

Hawthorne wrote Longfellow that he read his review "with huge delight." And he added that "whether or no the public will agree to the praise which you bestow on me, there are at least five persons who think you the most sagacious critic on earth—viz. my mother and two sisters, my old maiden aunt, and finally, the sturdiest believer of the whole five, my own self."

At last he had something he could take pride in. And with his own name on the title page! But the book sold only about nine hundred copies. His royalty rate was 10 percent of the retail price of one dollar. Although a critical success, commercially it was a flop. Still, it did more than win him praise. It would bring him a wife too.

A Love Affair

IN 1837 Hawthorne was thirty-three years old and still unmarried. Though shy, he was not without some experience of the opposite sex. His notebook jottings indicate that on his travels beyond Salem he had minor flirtations. But whether any affairs developed we don't know.

The one relationship that moved ahead was with Marianne Silsbee, the pretty daughter of a wealthy Salem merchant. She was twenty-eight when she met the local celebrity author in 1837. He had never known anyone like her and was charmed by this upper-class coquette. She flattered him and tried to make him open up to her his most intimate self. Always reserved, he resisted this approach.

But he continued to see Marianne, perhaps out of a selfish motive: Her father had considerable influence in Washington, and Hawthorne was pinning his hopes on a government job.

That year another Democratic administration took office in Washington. Martin Van Buren, Andrew Jackson's choice as his heir, entered the White House. Hawthorne's old friend Franklin

Pierce was now a senator, and another former classmate, Jonathan Cilley, a congressman. They scouted the federal agencies to find a spot for the struggling author.

Meanwhile, Salem, a town known for the liveliness of its gossip, buzzed with rumors of a Silsbee-Hawthorne love match.

In the summer of 1838, Marianne fell seriously sick, and visitors were denied her. Upon recovery, she asked Hawthorne to come see her. Though he did not encourage it, the rich heiress said that she would marry him—when he had an annual income of $3,000. His reply: Hardly likely!

A week later, Marianne married Jared Sparks, a much older man who had courted her long before. A recent widower, a Harvard professor, and a prominent historian, he would later become Harvard's president.

Months before this, another Salem woman had drawn Hawthorne's attention. She was Sophia Amelia Peabody. Her parents, Nathaniel Peabody, a dentist, and Elizabeth Palmer Peabody, a schoolteacher, had three girls and three boys. Sophia, the youngest daughter, five years younger than Hawthorne, had begun to write in childhood. But her real talent lay in painting and drawing. She suffered from frequent attacks of migraine headaches early on. Every drug the doctors could think of was tried on her. Though they did not cure, she managed to cope, and without losing her enduring optimism. Working so intensely at her art worsened her condition. Nevertheless, she studied chemistry and astronomy and mastered several foreign languages—Greek, Latin, Italian, Hebrew, and French.

A small, graceful woman, high spirited and generous, Sophia spoke in a low, sweet voice. She had often told her sisters that "nothing would ever tempt me to marry, and inflict upon a husband the care of such a sufferer."

It was Elizabeth, the oldest Peabody daughter, who introduced Hawthorne to Sophia in November 1837. Elizabeth, the same age

Although they had been neighbors as young children in Salem, Sophia Peabody, shown here at age thirty-six, was reintroduced to the writer through her sister Elizabeth in 1837.

as Nathaniel, was well known in New England for her progressive work in education, and she had become the friend of several of the region's writers. Of course she knew of *Twice-Told Tales*, for the author had sent her an inscribed copy, and she wanted to draw him into her circle. She induced him to join the Peabody sisters when they went to Miss Susan Burley's Saturday evening gatherings. It was a literary salon where people shared their common interests. After several such sessions he said he could not do without it.

The Peabody sisters, like almost all women of their day, were denied a college education. Their mother somehow found the energy to teach school while raising six children. Their father seems to have done little for them. She saw to it that her girls got a sound training in the major academic subjects as well as a deep understanding of ethical values. To waste time was a crime in her eyes, for God needed our action to fulfill moral obligations to ourselves and to the community. As she looked around her world, she saw extremes of poverty and wealth, with men so sure of their superiority they could exploit women without pity.

"I long for means and power to remedy this increasing misery," Mrs. Peabody said late in life, "but I wear petticoats and can never be Governor, Mayor, nor alderman, Judge or jury, senator or representative—so I may as well be quiet."

Elizabeth, the oldest daughter, never was quiet. To the end of her ninety years, she lived out her mother's credo, dedicated and tireless. She pioneered in early-childhood education through kindergarten schooling, and for years made her bookstore in Boston an intellectual center for writers, artists, and reformers. She fought for the abolition of slavery and the rights of the Native Americans.

Elizabeth never married. Her sister Mary married Horace Mann (1796–1859), who led the movement for better teaching and better pay for teachers. He became the first president of Antioch College in Ohio, where he demonstrated that coeducation can and does work.

The Peabodys believed Sophia would never marry. Yet Sophia said, "claims of the heart have great weight with me. I cannot be despondent for the universe, from all points, send arrows of light into my heart and mind. I really enjoy each thing." Hawthorne and Sophia's sisters took walks together, for she wasn't well enough to join them.

There was no proof yet that shy Nathaniel was serious about Sophia. Yet on her side, there were signs she was falling in love. He looked "very brilliant," she said after seeing him, and she had dreamed "about him all night." On another visit she reported that "he looked very handsome and full of smiles." Early in May, Sophia noted in her journal: "Oh! I forgot I never intended any one should have me for wife." Her sister Elizabeth, who probably wanted Hawthorne for herself, soon saw that Sophia was the right one to be made happy by him: "If there was ever a match made in Heaven, it was *that*."

It was a love affair that developed very slowly and through letters they exchanged. Just after seeing him out the door, Sophia could write him a nineteen-page letter, closing with a good night to her dear friend.

In his letters, his innate reserve begins to melt. He once thought, he told her, that he "could imagine all passions, all feelings, all states of the heart and mind." But she had taught him that he had a heart and had "revealed me to myself." Her innate optimism was a counterbalance to his gloomy disposition.

They would not marry for another four years. Meanwhile, if he was ever to be a caring husband and father, Hawthorne had to earn a much better living.

Justice,
Truth, and Love

IT WAS HIS FORMER CLASSMATE Jonathan Cilley who opened the way for Hawthorne to reach a broader audience. Cilley was a friend of John L. O'Sullivan, the brash young editor of the new *Democratic Review*. Urged by Cilley, the editor wrote Hawthorne, inviting him to contribute stories to the monthly magazine.

Politically, the magazine supported social reforms. In literature, it called for American writing of the highest quality. Hawthorne would be in good company, for O'Sullivan had enticed such leading writers as Longfellow, Whittier, Thoreau, Poe, Bryant, and Lowell to contribute. He offered higher rates—three to five dollars per page—than Hawthorne had ever seen before. Again, however, the money was slow in coming. Nevertheless, Hawthorne would continue writing for the magazine for many years.

O'Sullivan was a flamboyant character, bursting with energy and eager to speculate on all sorts of projects. Always short of

Jonathan Cilley, another Bowdoin classmate, aided Hawthorne's literary career by putting him in touch with the editor of the Democratic Review. *Cilley later died in a duel, shortly after taking office as the U.S. Representative from Maine.*

money to see them through, he earned a reputation as a con artist. After dealing with him for two years, Longfellow labeled him a "humbug."

O'Sullivan would befriend Hawthorne for nearly twenty years. When Sophia too was unable to resist his charm, Hawthorne admitted to her that despite the fact the editor was linked to some "foul companions" by "necessity and politics," there was less of the devil in him "than in other bipeds who wear breeches."

Neither *Twice-Told Tales* nor his work for O'Sullivan produced enough for Hawthorne—and a wife!—to live on. By now there was an understanding that he and Sophia would marry, but with no date set. In 1838 Longfellow suggested that he and Hawthorne collaborate on a book of fairy tales for young readers. The market for children's books was growing. Hawthorne hoped they would make "a great hit" and "entirely revolutionize the whole system of juvenile literature."

That fell through quickly when Longfellow changed his mind and wrote he would stick to poetry and translation. Maybe Longfellow was a bit wary of such a collaborator. To another friend, he wrote he found Hawthorne to be "a strange owl; a very peculiar individual, with a dash of originality about him, very pleasant to behold."

Meanwhile, friends were taking steps to find a government job for Hawthorne. One promising and exciting prospect was to have Hawthorne appointed official historian for the South Seas exploratory expedition of Lieutenant Charles Wilkes. Bridge, Cilley, Pierce, and O'Sullivan did their best in Washington, but nothing came of it. (The expedition would last from 1838 to 1842, and discover that Antarctica was a continent.)

Then Elizabeth Peabody stepped in. Approaching her friend Orestes Brownson, recently appointed to the Custom House in Boston, she got him to speak to George Bancroft, an American historian and a major figure in the Democratic Party of Massachusetts with great influence on political appointments.

It worked. Hawthorne was given the job of measurer of coal at the Custom House, for $1,500 a year. This was not to be his only political job. He would never make enough from his literary work to support a family. There would always be the pressing need to do something else to earn a dollar.

As it turned out, he learned how to navigate in the political waters of the Democratic Party. One of the reasons he identified with this party was because his college friends had been Democrats. Plus, he had no love for the snooty Whigs (the opposing party of that era) he knew in Salem. He favored the plain people, Andrew Jackson's followers, while he seemed blind to Jackson's racist views of Indians and blacks.

While waiting for the Custom House job to come through, Hawthorne discussed with the Massachusetts Board of Education plans for a children's history of the United States. They liked the idea, and he began working on the book. His publisher was a newcomer in the field—E. P. Peabody—Sophia's enterprising sister Elizabeth. She had already been publishing pamphlets for reform groups, such as the American Anti-Slavery Society. With little money to sustain her, she had the courage and the confidence in Sophia's man to move ahead.

The title was *Grandfather's Chair: A History for Youth*. Meant for easy reading by children, it was just 3 by 5 inches (8 by 13 centimeters), 140 pages, with no illustrations.

Hawthorne built his account of American history during colonial days (including Salem's witchcraft craze) upon the passage of an old oak chair from one historical figure to a series of others. The storyteller is a grandfather. Circled by his grandchildren, he tells them what happened and why and how, and they cut in now and then with questions and comments.

Keeping to the format of little books, Hawthorne took two more volumes to bring the history to the year 1808, with the new nation up and running. The first volume appeared in December 1840, with *Famous Old People* out two months later, and *Liberty Tree* in March 1841.

Nearing the end of the story, Hawthorne has grandfather's chair itself speak, telling the children, "As long as I have stood in the midst of human affairs I have constantly observed that Justice, Truth and Love are the chief ingredients of every happy life."

A year later, Hawthorne followed these books with *Biographical Stories for Children*. Here a father tells his blind son about the lives of great people such as Benjamin Franklin, Sir Isaac Newton, and Queen Christina of Sweden. Printed in small editions at about fifty cents each, royalties added little to his income.

That same year, 1842, a second edition of *Twice-Told Tales* was published, with Hawthorne adding twenty-one pieces. The sales were so poor that Hawthorne said, "I wish the devil had the books, for I suppose he is a member of the Trade."

Measurer of Coal and Salt

MEASURER OF coal and salt. It sounds like an odd sort of job for a teller of tales. And it was. But it paid Hawthorne a salary of $1,500 a year, a good salary for those days. Added to it were the fees he drew for every cargo of salt and coal he measured. In his first year on the job, these brought his income up to $2,000. While working at the Custom House, he rented a parlor and bedroom in the Boston home of George Hillard, a friend of the Peabody sisters. He walked to work in the morning, and coming home in the evening would sit by the fireside and write long letters to Sophia, to whom he was now secretly engaged.

His duties kept him outdoors most of the time, measuring the big tubs of coal and salt as they were unloaded from the ship onto the docks. In winter weather, icy winds had him moving fast to keep from freezing. Or he would nip into the cabin of one of the incoming schooners and have a cup of hot tea, sitting on a biscuit barrel and warming himself by the hot stove. When quarrels broke out between captains and work gangs, his job was to

54

settle them. You should see how awfully stern I can look, he wrote Sophia. If the weather was too harsh to work, or no ships entered the harbor, he killed time by reading the papers or tuning in to the buzz of conversation among the port officers.

His patron, George Bancroft, told friends that Hawthorne "was the best and most efficient of the Custom House officers." When off duty, Hawthorne visited art galleries, read in the library of the Boston Athenaeum, or walked on Boston Commons— declaring, "blessed be God for this green tract." He felt, he said, doomed to murder time at that unblest Custom House "that makes such havoc with my wits."

Through his connections, Hawthorne was able to land a good-paying job at the Boston Custom House in 1839. The building was the most expensive and elaborate custom house in the nation, and in its time was known as the greatest building in Boston.

He wrote Sophia that his external life on the docks was dry and dull, but internally, in his thoughts and feelings, he was savoring the joyous times they would have together. "Nobody would think that the same man could live two such different lives simultaneously."

Those letters to Sophia "are the letters of a man so deeply and happily in love that every quality he possesses glows for the first time in its fullest strength. They are passionate, they are delicate, and they are humorous," said the scholar Mark Van Doren. Sophia's letters, too, must have been equally expressive, although few survive as Hawthorne burned them later on when they went to England. "It is astonishing how much more I love thee every day," she says in one of the few we have.

Hawthorne continued to write in his journal, recording events of the day, odd characters he observed, the scenes on the waterfront: "Objects on a wharf—a huge pile of cotton bales from a New Orleans ship, twenty or thirty feet high, as high as a house. Barrels of molasses, in regular ranges; casks of linseed oil. Iron in bars landing from a vessel . . . Long Wharf is devoted to ponderous, evil-smelling, inelegant necessaries of life."

Among those "inelegant necessaries" was cheap immigrant labor. One day an English ship pulled in to unload "seventy or thereabouts factory girls, imported to work in our factories, some pale and delicate-looking, others ragged and coarse."

Hawthorne made no comment on how these young immigrants were exploited. The agents of New England textile mills brought them in to work fourteen to sixteen hours a day for a wage of about $1.50 a week. The industrialists were ruthless in their pressure for lowest cost and highest profit.

Hawthorne told Longfellow he was saying good-bye to literature, "for as a literary man my new occupations entirely break me up." And when O'Sullivan asked why he hadn't sent in pieces, he replied, "The fact is I am quite done for and broken up as a literary man, so long as I retain this office." He added, "If ever I come

New England textile mills, like this cotton mill in Lowell, Massachusetts (above), *proliferated in the mid-1800s. Many young, female immigrants who came through the port of Boston where Hawthorne oversaw customs were destined to be hired as cheap labor for the mills.*

to be worth $5000 I will kick all business to the devil—at least till that be spent."

Yet he did at times find that his work stirred his literary juices:

On board my salt-vessels and colliers there are many things happening, many pictures which, in future years, when I am again busy at the loom of fiction, I could weave in; but my fancy is rendered so torpid by my ungenial way of life that I cannot sketch off the scenes and portraits that interest me, and I am forced to trust them to my memory, with the hope of recalling them at a more favorable period.

In 1840 the Peabodys moved from Salem to Boston. Now Hawthorne could enjoy Sophia's company directly. It was her sister Elizabeth who brought the family to live above her new bookshop on 11 West Street. While she sold books and magazines there, one of her brothers ran his pharmacy in a corner. Sophia did not work in the store but in her own upstairs studio room. Her copies of old masterworks of art were displayed for sale in the parlor below.

Every Wednesday at eleven in the morning, as many as thirty women met in the bookshop to take part in Margaret Fuller's "Conversations." Fuller (1810–1850) lead with a brief introduction to some theme: Hindu mythology, Greek civilization, education, health, the fine arts, ethics, and—dearest to her heart—the rights of women. She led the women like a virtuoso conductor, opening the way for them to ask questions and offer their own ideas or criticism. Taking part in these sessions, said the reformer Thomas Wentworth Higginson, "were the most alert and active-minded women in Boston."

Sophia, however, did not join in Fuller's Conversations. Was she too shy? Or did she feel uncomfortable in the presence of so brilliant a woman? Neither she nor Hawthorne could be blind to what was going on in the Boston of those years. The city was electric with new ideas, fresh insights into society, and the need for change. It was that ferment that would lead Hawthorne to try something new.

Portrait of
Margaret Fuller

How to describe Margaret Fuller? She was author, editor, critic, columnist, teacher, feminist, war correspondent—the pioneer of another and better world for women. Quite a catalog of achievement for a woman who would live only to the age of forty. Her father, Timothy Fuller, was a Massachusetts lawyer and congressperson. At a time when women were treated as second-class citizens, he was determined that his firstborn child be educated to fulfill her natural talents. As soon as she could talk, she was trained in languages, history, and literature. It led to widening and deepening her experience with gifted men and women. During her years teaching school, she got to know Elizabeth Peabody and launched the famous Conversations at the Boston bookshop. With Emerson she edited the *Dial*, a journal voicing the Transcendental belief in the free life of the spirit. Later she joined Horace Greeley's paper, the *New York Tribune*, where she became a powerful critic of literature. She also investigated social conditions in prisons and welfare institutions and campaigned for reforms. Greeley sent her to Europe as his foreign correspondent, where she covered Italy's struggle for freedom in 1848. It was there she would meet the Hawthornes again. She, her Italian husband, and their child died in a shipwreck off Fire Island, New York, in 1850.

Trying Out Utopia

IN JANUARY 1841, Hawthorne resigned from his job at the Boston Custom House. "I have broken my chains and escaped," he told Longfellow. He knew he'd lose the job anyway because the Democrats had lost the election of 1840 to the Whigs. And, as usual, the spoils of office would go to their followers. He told Sophia he detested all offices held through political connections. "Politicians," he said, "are not men; they cease to be men in becoming politicians."

Much as he claimed he detested that job, he had tried his best to get all he could out of it. He had made enough money—for the first time!—to support himself and was even able to pile up a safety cushion. Out of his savings, he generously loaned money to O'Sullivan and two workers at the Custom House.

What to do next?

Emerson's followers, the Transcendentalists, believed harmony—not conflict, not war of class against class—would bring lasting peace. It was a time of optimism, of faith in the perfectibility of one's self, if only you tried hard enough. Instead of thinking of ways to improve society, the Transcendentalists' focus was inward. As Emerson wrote in his book *Nature* (1836), "If the single man plant himself indomitably on his instincts, and there abide, the huge world will come round to him." Margaret Fuller's friends were buzzing with the new ideas. Couldn't you improve your own life? Earn your living without crippling your soul? Escape the dog-eat-dog competition? The goal was self-sufficiency.

Others had dreamed of a better life long ago. Back in 1516, a book called *Utopia* by Sir Thomas More had been published. He pictured an ideal society where everyone cooperated to provide the best for all, and where such evils as poverty and injustice were eliminated. In future years the name Utopia would be applied to schemes for other ideal states.

By the mid-1800s, time many were worrying about the grim effects of the new Industrial Revolution. The move from farm to factory had disturbed old ways of living. People in the mills were overworked and underpaid, shut off from the countryside and traditional customs. In 1841 several thinking this way decided to seek an escape from all this by creating a Utopian community at Brook Farm in West Roxbury, 9 miles (14 kilometers) from Boston. It was a dairy farm of about 170 acres (70 hectares) with ample green pastures and pinewoods. Promoting the scheme was George Ripley, formerly a Unitarian minister. To finance the project, a joint-stock company was formed, with twenty-four shares offered to members at $500 a share. Each member would do part of the manual labor needed to feed and house the group.

The Brook Farmers wanted their style of living to serve as a model for society at large. Ripley aimed at building an ideal community that would allow people to use their minds and do menial labor as well, so that everyone would have the benefit of education as well as the satisfaction of physical work.

George Ripley organized and headed Brook Farm in the 1840s. The society was founded on the ideals of a communal, Utopian living experience.

The major purpose was to free the individual at least partially from the pressures of society. In theory, its members would earn their living by spending the mornings working for the community on the farm chores, in the barns, the dormitories, or taking part in its various money-earning projects. The afternoons they could devote to creative work—such as writing or painting. And their evenings would be social occasions. The artist—whether in words or paint or music—could thus devote nearly half his or her time to their craft and still be assured of a living.

Clearly Hawthorne did not share the excited optimism of those who invested their hopes and their dollars in Brook Farm. He once said that "a man has no claim upon his fellow creatures, beyond bread and water, and a grave, unless he can win it by his own strength and skill."

It is odd, then, that he joined the project in April 1841, investing $1,000 of his savings in the joint stock—one $500 share for himself, one for Sophia. He probably did it because he hoped the Brook Farm cooperative would provide the means for supporting a wife. They had now been engaged for two years and still had no solid footing for marriage. He told Sophia he was going "to prepare a home for my Dove, and will return for her, all in good time."

Hawthorne arrived at Brook Farm on a snowy day in mid-April. He found only a farmhouse and a few outbuildings. Across the road was a house rented to serve as a school for the colony's children. He met some twenty other members. (By the end of his short stay, there would be fifty.) Soon two wings were added for use as parlor, sitting room, a day nursery, men's dormitory, and laundry. The daily schedule: rise at 4:30, breakfast at 6:30, dine at 12:30, to bed at 9.

In those early months, Hawthorne joined the men in farm labor while the women did the household chores. He liked it, he wrote Sophia: "Such a delectable way of life has never been seen

Josiah Walcott painted this view of Brook Farm in 1844. Hawthorne lived at the farm from April to November of 1841.

on earth, since the days of the early Christians." His job was to milk the cows, the "kindliest" ones, he hoped. He chopped hay for the cattle so vigorously that he broke the machine. He carried in wood, relit the fires, and then sat down "and ate up a huge mound of buckwheat cakes." Next, armed with a pitchfork, he made "a gallant attack upon a heap of manure." The time on the manure pile left him "stinking so badly you wouldn't want to come within a half-mile of me."

When the weather went bad, he caught a severe cold that kept him in bed for several days. He felt isolated, reading no newspapers and knowing no more of what was going on "than if I dwelt on another planet." But with true spring blossoming, he found Brook Farm more and more beautiful. In late May, Sophia visited briefly and said she was "enchanted" with it. "Most joyously could I dwell there for its own beauty's sake." And then, closing, she wrote, "It is astonishing how much more I love thee every day."

But after a couple of months, Hawthorne's enthusiasm began to fade. He found that farm life made it just as hard to write as the Custom House. "It is my opinion," he wrote Sophia, "that a man's soul may be buried and perish under a dung-heap, or in a furrow of the field, just as well as under a pile of money." His sister Louisa wrote, chiding him for never coming for a visit and asking, "What is the use of burning your brains out in the sun, when you can do anything better with them?"

Near the end of August, Hawthorne wrote Sophia that he was now doubting that Brook Farm was the right place to start their married life. There were problems about the deed to the land, and Ripley was having trouble raising enough money to keep the colony going.

Meanwhile, Hawthorne was trying to get his pen moving. Would a new edition of *Grandfather's Chair*, adding more stories and drawings by Sophia, be the way out of Brook Farm? No, he mustn't fool himself. How could he expect much from the future when his past literary efforts had earned so little? He said wistfully that other such "little books" as he meant to write had "bought large estates and built mansions." Maybe his efforts could at least "enable me to build a little cottage or at least to buy or hire one?"

Now he was looking to Sophia for help, asking her to criticize his stories in draft form. And when she questioned three of them, pointing out faults, he kept them out of the second volume of *Twice-Told Tales*. We don't know what she disliked for her letters have not survived.

Late that September at Brook Farm, Hawthorne switched from laborer to merely boarder. That gave him time to write—but nothing came. He didn't have "the sense of perfect seclusion which has always been essential to my power of producing anything." Well, not to worry. Meantime he would try to decide whether the colony was the right place for him and Sophia "to cast in our lot among them."

Even though now a boarder, Hawthorne pitched in to help with the harvesting of potatoes and apples. One bright afternoon in late September, everyone stopped work to enjoy a picnic and costume party celebrating a child's birthday. Emerson and Margaret Fuller came as guests, delighting in the sight of colonists in their fabulous costumes prancing wildly in the woods, while Hawthorne lay under the trees in his favorite role of observer.

In November 1841, after eight months at Brook Farm, Hawthorne left. Later, he sued for the recovery of a loan he had made Ripley shortly before his resignation. Though he won the case, he never got his money back.

What about marriage? It is hard to believe that after some two years considering themselves engaged, they had still not told his family. Hawthorne reassured Sophia: The Hawthornes all liked her, no doubt of it. But they were reserved about emotional matters. They never talked of their deepest feelings. "I cannot take my heart in my hand, and show it to them," he said.

Adam and Eve

AT LAST, Hawthorne stopped stalling. He and Sophia set a date for the wedding in June. He told his mother and sisters, and Sophia wrote them so sweet a letter that Hawthorne said, "If they do not love thee, it will be because they have no hearts to love with."

As June began, Sophia's headaches returned, and the ceremony had to be put off until July 9. That day the sun brightened the parlor of her parents, where the Peabodys gathered to witness the marriage. Hawthorne's sisters did not attend.

As soon as it was over, the newlyweds left by carriage for their home in Concord. They had rented the Old Manse, a gray parsonage built in 1770 for the Reverend William Emerson (Ralph Waldo's grandfather) and then taken over by the Reverend Ezra Ripley, who had recently died. From the window of the upstairs study, you could see the North Bridge, where the Minutemen had fired on British troops, starting the American Revolution. Only five years before Hawthorne's marriage, Emerson had written his "Concord Hymn" for the dedication of the Battle Monument.

The newlywed Hawthornes made their first home together in the Old Manse in Concord, Massachusetts, a building that would be immortalized in Hawthorne's story collection, Mosses from an Old Manse.

Behind the parsonage was an apple orchard, with currant bushes and cherry and pear trees adding to the bounty of fruit. Neighbor Henry David Thoreau had planted a vegetable garden for the parsonage—beans, Indian corn, and squash—gifts for the new couple.

The house, furnished, was theirs for an annual rental of $100. To the old-fashioned beds, chairs, and chests, Hawthorne added his simple belongings for use in his upstairs study. Fearful of their frail daughter being overworked, the Peabodys had hired a young Irish woman to work for the newlyweds. "We are Adam and Eve," Sophia told her mother. "I am the happiest person on earth."

During their first weeks in the Old Manse, they redecorated the rooms—fresh paint, wallpaper, a new carpet for the parlor, and a new cookstove. Grim old portraits on the walls were removed and stored in the attic. Concord neighbors, a friendly lot, dropped by to welcome them. They noted such events in a journal they began to keep jointly, teasing one another in their entries. Hawthorne was so happy he didn't feel much like writing anything. "What is there to write about at all? Happiness has no succession of events." Sometimes he left their bed at five in the morning to fish for bream and perch in the muddy Concord River. A lucky catch would put food on the breakfast or dinner table.

Breakfast over, he took care of the garden, overwhelmed by its plenty. Then up to his study. No serious writing yet, only jottings in the journal and long stretches of reading. After their midday dinner came the happiest part of the day, a walk with Sophia.

Sometimes he walked to Walden Pond, alone or with a friend, to swim in its sparkling blue water. It did not only his

A view from Henry David Thoreau's house on Walden Pond, where Hawthorne would enjoy summer swims. The Hawthornes and Thoreau were neighbors and friends.

Thoreau (left) *and Ralph Waldo Emerson* (right) *were a part of the literary community in Concord, where Hawthorne lived.*

body good, he said, but his "moral self to receive a cleansing from that bath."

It was an extraordinary chapter in America's literary history that so many famous writers should have lived in one tiny town, Concord, with a population then of only two thousand people. Thoreau was born there; Emerson came because it was the home of his ancestors. Hawthorne came chiefly because he was offered the Old Manse for a home. Bronson Alcott (father of Louisa May Alcott) came to be near Emerson. As did Margaret Fuller.

One day Thoreau came to dine with the Hawthornes at midday. For dessert there was the first watermelon from the garden. After dinner the two men walked along the riverbank until they came to Thoreau's small rowboat, green with a border of blue. It was called the *Musketaquid*, an Indian name meaning "the river of meadows." It was the boat in which Thoreau and his brother John had spent a week on the Concord and Merrimac rivers.

Hawthorne and Thoreau boarded, with Thoreau rowing upstream with great ease, a skill he had learned from watching Indians paddling their canoes.

Because Thoreau needed money, he sold the boat to Hawthorne for seven dollars. The new owner wryly commented that he wished he "could acquire the acquatic skill of the original owner at as reasonable a rate." The next day, Thoreau gave Hawthorne a lesson in paddling.

In his journal, Hawthorne tried to capture the unique personality of Thoreau:

> He is a singular character—a young man with much of wild original nature still remaining in him; and so far as he is sophisticated, it is in a way and method of his own. He is as ugly as sin, long-nosed, queer-mouthed, and with uncouth and somewhat rustic, although courteous manners, corresponding very well with such an exterior. But his ugliness is of an honest and agreeable fashion, and becomes him much better than beauty. . . . Mr. Thorow [sic] is a keen and delicate observer of nature . . . and Nature, in return for his love, seems to adopt him as her special child, and shows him secrets which few others are allowed to witness. . . .

Admiring Thoreau's writing, Hawthorne would recommend him to editors who had published his own pieces.

We have another word portrait of the Concord neighbors— Hawthorne, Emerson, and Thoreau—from the pen of Sophia. When winter came, she watched them skating on the Concord River and painted this sensitive picture:

> One afternoon, Mr. Emerson and Mr. Thoreau went with him down the river. Henry Thoreau is an experienced skater, and was figuring dithyrambic dances and Bacchic

> leaps on the ice—very remarkable, but very ugly, methought. Next to him followed Mr. Hawthorne who, wrapped in his cloak, moved like a self-impelled Greek statue, stately, and grave. Mr. Emerson closed the line, evidently too weary to hold himself erect, pitching headforemost, half lying on the air. He came in to rest himself, and said to me that Hawthorne was a tiger, a bear, a lion,—in short, a satyr, and there was no tiring him out; and he might be the death of a man like himself.

Emerson wanted to make Concord a center for thinkers and writers, to break down the isolation so many suffered from. He invited Hawthorne to join him on a walking trip of some 20 miles (32 kilometers) to Harvard, Massachusetts, to visit a Shaker village. They were gone two days in late September, but Hawthorne's journal notes only that he had missed his wife. Emerson kept trying to break through Hawthorne's reserve, to little effect. Sophia noted that Emerson would continue to talk and talk and get only a smile from Hawthorne. Each man would send the other his books as they appeared, but it is doubtful they read one another deeply. They remained good neighbors, never intimate friends.

The winter of 1842–1843 was one of the coldest in Concord for twenty years. Every day after breakfast, Hawthorne worked in his study till two o'clock. The stories he was writing began to appear in James Russell Lowell's new magazine, *The Pioneer*. (Between then and 1845, he would write twenty stories.) After dinner at two, he walked to the post office to see if there was mail, then to the Concord Athenaeum, where he would read till sunset. The long winter evenings he spent with Sophia. He marveled that she who had once lived among a large circle of friends could now be content to have him as her sole companion.

John O'Sullivan was one of their rare visitors that winter. "No friend is dearer to Mr. Hawthorne than he," Sophia told her mother, and he says we have "the happiest house in the world." One evening in February, the Hawthornes went walking on the frozen Concord River. Sophia, who was pregnant with their first child, slipped and fell. The result of the accident was a miscarriage.

They each hoped to take the short trip to visit their respective families in Boston and Salem. Lack of money held them up. The magazines rarely paid Hawthorne promptly for his pieces. Somehow, enough came in for them to make their trips in March. Apart for only a few days, each missed the other terribly.

During the winter, Hawthorne wrote Longfellow to invite him to lecture at the Concord Lyceum. It would pay ten dollars. The poet declined, however. Hawthorne himself refused to give a talk, even though he badly needed the fee. Longfellow's new book, *Poems on Slavery*, had just come out. Before reading it, Hawthorne wrote that he was surprised by the subject, for the poet had never tackled such a burning issue before. It was an issue Hawthorne himself shied away from, even as it dominated political life.

One day, when in Cambridge, Hawthorne dined with the Longfellows. Mrs. Longfellow noted in her journal that "Hawthorne has a fine manly head but is the most shy and silent of men. The freest conversation did not thaw forth more than a monosyllable and we discussed art glibly enough. I really pity a person under this spell of reserve. . . ."

That spring Sophia's sister Mary married Horace Mann. They sailed to Europe on a honeymoon to be combined with Mann's study of European schools. Sophia went to Boston to visit family, leaving Hawthorne at home alone. It was a hard time for him, although Emerson, Thoreau, and others made calls. Hawthorne noted that Emerson thought Margaret Fuller the greatest woman of her time.

Hawthorne kept in touch with Horatio Bridge. When Bridge signed on as purser on a warship that would cruise West African waters for two years, Hawthorne asked him to write reports about his experiences for a book that Hawthorne would edit for him. He confided to Bridge that he was so short of money he sometimes "sighed for the regular monthly payments at the Custom House."

When Bridge sent him graphic descriptions of what he was seeing on the voyage, Hawthorne replied with notes on how he might do even better. His ideas could be useful to any aspiring writer:

> I would advise you not to stick too accurately to the bare fact, either in your descriptions or your narrations; else your hand will be cramped, and the result will be a want of freedom, that will deprive you of a higher truth than that which you strive to attain. Allow your fancy pretty free license, and omit no heightening touches merely because they did not chance to happen before your eyes. If they did not happen, they at least ought—which is all that concerns you.

This is a clue to Hawthorne's readiness to blur the difference between fact and fiction in his own work. He goes on:

> If you meet with any distinguished characters, give personal sketches of them. Begin to write always before the impression of novelty has worn off your mind; else you will begin to think that the peculiarities which at first attracted you, are not worth recording. Think nothing too trifling to write down, so it be in the smallest degree characteristic.

A year after the Hawthornes' wedding, they were happy that Sophia was pregnant again. Their daughter Una was born on March 3, 1844. She "roars very lustily," Hawthorne reported to his sister. A father for the first time at the age of forty, he found it brought on "a very sober and serious kind of happiness . . . I have business on earth now. . . ."

He began writing longer hours. He didn't find that it used up his strength. "I might have written more," he confided to his journal, "if it had seemed worthwhile." He meant those twenty short sketches and tales he produced in 1843–1844 were barely enough to support the family. And he couldn't expect to do any better at the writing trade.

Then what could he hope for?

Another government job?

12

The Fragrance of Flowers

THE INTENSE PRESSURE to make just a bare living never let up. Hawthorne kept pushing his friend O'Sullivan to help him find a government post. Maybe as Salem postmaster? The editor tried, pulling strings with one influential man after another. He's a fine writer, a credit to American literature, he's married with a second child coming, can't support the family by his pen, surely he deserves government aid!

Nothing worked. It would be another three years before a political appointment came through. Although O'Sullivan's *Democratic Review* was not prospering, Hawthorne continued to send it his best work, such as the allegorical fable, "The Celestial Railroad." To other magazines, especially those catering to female readers, he sent his lesser pieces. Those readers were so used to reading diluted trash that in his opinion they wouldn't know good stuff when they saw it. Even when published, little came back in payment.

The biographer James R. Mellow points out that Hawthorne in some of these stories makes a stereotype of certain characters.

75

Especially the female reformer. In "The Christmas Banquet," perhaps with Margaret Fuller or his sister-in-law Elizabeth Peabody in mind, he describes the feminist as "a woman of unemployed energy, who finds herself in the world with nothing to achieve, nothing to enjoy and nothing even to suffer. She had, therefore, driven herself to the verge of madness by dark brooding over the wrongs of her sex, and its exclusion from a proper field of actions."

It was bad enough to lack money for Sophia, Una, and himself; his family in Salem could use help too. Yet here he was, a man of forty, and unable to help anyone.

He pinned his hopes on the coming presidential election. If the Democrat James Polk were elected, he was sure he'd have a regular income from a government job. Otherwise, what? Not

Hawthorne hoped that his custom-house experience and loyalty to the Democratic Party would result in a lucrative government appointment upon the election of Democrat James Polk (left) as president in 1844. Although a position did eventually come through, the financially beleaguered Hawthorne had to wait two years.

BY
NATHANIEL HAWTHORNE

BOSTON AND NEW YORK:
HOUGHTON, MIFFLIN AND COMPANY.
The Riverside Press, Cambridge.
1887.

The title page of Mosses from an Old Manse, *published in 1887. The first edition was published in 1846. A second edition, which included four additional stories, among them "Rappaccini's Daughter," followed in 1854.*

more stories, for which he was so poorly paid, if at all. Only hack-work—translations, schoolbooks, whatever.

With Polk the winner in November 1844, Hawthorne thought his troubles would soon end. But the machinery of political patronage moved slowly. Meanwhile, six months passed without his being able to pay a penny of his rent. That fall the owner of the Old Manse, the late Reverend Ripley's son, decided to take it over for himself. In October 1845, the Hawthornes left Concord to move into Hawthorne's mother's house in Salem. With only ten dollars in his pocket, he was taking a chance on finding a job there.

In 1846, soon after he left Concord, Hawthorne's collection of stories, *Mosses from an Old Manse*, was published. There were twenty-three pieces, seventeen of them written in the Old Manse. Three were among his best—"Roger Malvin's Burial," "Young

The literary greats of Hawthorne's time, including Edgar Allan Poe (left) *and poet William Cullen Bryant* (right), *recognized and praised Hawthorne's outstanding talents as a writer.*

Goodman Brown," and "Rappaccini's Daughter"—created earlier but left out of previous volumes.

By this time, notable critics were praising the fine quality of Hawthorne's work. Poe said his "distinctive trait is invention, creation, imagination, originality—a trait which, in the literature of fiction is positively worth all the rest." And William Cullen Bryant said his was "the best written" English on either side of the Atlantic.

The concern of Hawthorne's Concord friends for contemporary issues was reflected in his recent work. In one piece, "The New Adam and Eve," he said the lust for gold was "the very essence of the system that had wrought itself into the vitals of mankind and choked their original nature in its deadly grip." The bleak contrast between classes in America—the few "rolling in luxury, while the multitude was toiling for scanty food," he denounced as a "great and miserable fact."

In another piece, "The Procession of Life," Hawthorne recognizes the "apostles of humanity" whose campaigns for social reform reached in "the prison, the insane asylum, the squalid chambers of the almshouse, the manufactory where the demon of machinery annihilates the human soul, the cotton field where God's image becomes a beast of burden, and every other scene where man wrongs or neglects his brother."

Yet what result could reformers hope for? Hawthorne clung to the Puritan belief that no better world will come about until our mortal souls are purified. Meanwhile, he wrote in "The Hall of Fantasy," we should enjoy

> the fragrance of flowers and of new-mown hay; the genial warmth of sunshine and the beauty of a sunset among clouds; the comfort and cheerful glow of the fireside; the deliciousness of fruits and of all good cheer; the magnificence of mountains and seas and cataracts, and the softer charm of rural scenery; even the fast falling snow and the gray atmosphere through which it descends . . . the country frolics; the homely humor; the broad, open-mouthed roar of laughter, in which body and soul conjoin so heartily! I fear that no other world can show us anything just like this.

As he sweated out the wait for a political appointment, he borrowed more than once from his generous friend Bridge. Not until April 1846 did President Polk stamp his approval on Hawthorne's appointment as surveyor of the port of Salem. The salary was $1,200 a year. Hawthorne did not feel that it was a great living, but it was enough to be comfortable and it would leave him time for his writing.

Manifest Destiny

As the 1840s began, the total population of the United States was 17 million, including almost 3 million African Americans. The part of the continent which comprised the nation was only thinly settled. (Today, New York State alone has 19 million people.) The nation held twenty-six states. It was still an infant nation, the great majority in the North living on farms owned by the families that worked them. In the South, large plantations predominated, with slaves working them.

The cry for expanding the borders of the nation was in full chorus. Many dreamed of tilling their own farms out west, while others dreamed of founding new fortunes by speculating in land. To merchants and manufacturers, the prospect of expanded borders meant new markets for their goods and services.

There were ideas aplenty to justify expansion. But the most effective was to claim that expansion was America's "manifest destiny." And it was Hawthorne's editor and friend, John L. O'Sullivan, who coined that phrase. His magazine, the *Democratic Review*, proclaimed that our national mission was to spread American democracy across the North American continent.

Expansion would have been easy if nothing had been in the way. It quickly turned out that war was the price of expansion. And expansion was thoroughly entangled with the issue of slavery. Many saw it as a plot to create new slave states and thus further to expand the South's power in national affairs.

It was the election of James Polk, the Democratic presidential candidate, on an expansionist platform that opened the way into the Mexican War. It was the first successful offensive war in American history. The first time American forces had occupied an enemy capitol. The first time the United States had ruled under

This mural in Los Angeles, California, pictures Mexican and U.S negotiators signing the Treaty of Guadalupe Hidalgo, ending the Mexican War (1846–1848) in February 1848.

martial law on foreign soil. And a war that many people, like Ulysses S. Grant, who fought in it, thought the most disgraceful war the country ever fought (up to that time).

By the peace treaty imposed on the Mexicans, the United States acquired about 850,000 square miles (over 2 million square kilometers) or one-third of Mexico's land—more than the combined area of France, Spain, and Italy.

What Hawthorne thought of it all—the slogan O'Sullivan created, the war his Democratic Party maneuvered—we don't know. He was silent, or at least he left no record of his thinking.

The Salem Custom House

WHEN HAWTHORNE reported for duty at the Salem Custom House, the port had been decaying for some time. Many ships preferred to dock at the deep-water ports of Boston or New York these days. Yet in his first week on duty, twenty-one ships arrived at the port, so it was surely not dead. His work took up mornings only. There were many more people on staff than were needed, not uncommon in government offices. From his tall desk on the ground floor, he could see the wharves and harbor. A few blocks away was the house he had been born in.

His job was to supervise the work of eight inspectors, dispatching them to the incoming ships to collect the taxes on imports. He signed the official papers. His name was stamped on all the bags, baskets, boxes, and bales that carried dutiable merchandise.

It was Hawthorne's habit to claim he had nothing to do on this job. But it took a hardworking and conscientious official to carry out the tasks. It wasn't easy to be honest, for the whole customs service was infected by the same corruption that messed up the national political life.

Most of the people around him knew nothing of his writing. He sometimes wondered whether those who came across his name stamped on merchandise carried to all corners of the world knew if that name meant anything in literature.

Through side windows, he could see old seamen hanging around the waterfront. He referred to his subordinate officers, who were often snoozing in their tipped-back chairs in the central hallways, as patriarchal veterans. They spun tales of the dim past. Did any know the tales he had written?

In June, soon after he started the new job, his second child, Julian, was born. That fall the Hawthornes moved into a small house on Chestnut Street. Longfellow, who had commissioned

Hawthorne worked in this office at the Salem Custom House from 1847 until 1849.

*In 1846 Hawthorne posed for this portrait by well-
known portrait artist Eastman Johnson. The picture,
along with others, resides in the Longfellow National
Historic Site in Cambridge, Massachusetts.*

the artist Eastman Johnson to do portraits of his family and
friends, got Hawthorne to sit for his. Sophia felt that her forty-
two-year-old husband had never looked so handsome.

Yes, he had a steady job, but not a steady income. The Custom
House fees were quite small, and whatever was due him the government was extremely slow in paying.

Now and then, he saw old college friends. While still living in
Concord, Pierce and Bridge had visited him. With the Mexican
War under way in 1846, Pierce had been appointed a colonel and
then, in 1847, moved up to brigadier general. Hawthorne went to

Boston that March to see Pierce off as he took command of several regiments boarding ship en route to the Mexican front.

In their small house, there was no private space for Hawthorne to isolate himself and write. He watched anxiously for sales reports on the two-volume edition of *Mosses from an Old Manse*. Six small editions appeared over a period of years, but the royalties never amounted to much.

In September 1847, the Hawthornes found a large house in Salem at 14 Mall Street for a rental of $200 a year. Three stories high, it had a separate group of rooms that Hawthorne's mother and sisters would move into. Each side of the family had the privacy it needed. Hawthorne's mother enjoyed her grandchildren, and Louisa took care of them when Hawthorne and Sophia went out for a walk.

A third-floor study gave the author ample room to write. Only he did little of that. When mornings at the Custom House ended, he went to his study—to dream about stories, he said, but somehow not to write them. In his three years as port surveyor, he produced only one good story for publication, "Ethan Brand." Plus a minor historical sketch, "Main Street," which Elizabeth Peabody ran in the first—and only!—issue of her publication, *Aesthetic Papers*. That May 1849 issue made an enduring mark, however, because it also contained Thoreau's essay, "Resistance to Civil Government," later famous as "Civil Disobedience." A lecture in its first form, it came out of Thoreau's resistance to the war America was waging against Mexico. He had been jailed overnight in Concord for his refusal to pay taxes financing what he saw as an unjust war. His was a radical view of conscientious objection. He believed each citizen had an obligation to disobey a law that would violate his conscience. Thus he would awaken fellow citizens to a wrong and make them willing to correct it. That doctrine would move people around the world to act against war and tyranny. Two hundred years later, Mahatma Gandhi in

Elizabeth Peabody, shown here in the 1850s, published her Aesthetic Papers, *which included a piece by Hawthorne. Peabody supported many progressive ideals including education reform, abolition of slavery, and women's suffrage.*

India turned it into mass moral pressure for gaining social and political goals. And Martin Luther King Jr., during the struggle for civil rights, would respond in his way to the words uttered in Concord long before.

Hawthorne also wrote a few book reviews during this period. In one of them, he praised *Typee*, a new novel by an unknown writer, Herman Melville, who would become his friend.

When Una was four and Julian two, Hawthorne began noting in his journal what they said and did. For more than a year, he took delight in describing his children—how they dressed, the games they played, their babble. He entered into their play and made up stories for them. Try as he might, he couldn't keep up with them. "Una has just come in," he wrote at one moment, "and puts me so far behind my subject that I am almost tempted to give up in despair."

Whenever Sophia and the children were away on visits, he was miserable. "I cannot bear the loneliness of the house," he wrote

Hawthorne took great delight in his children, Julian (left) *and Una* (right). *This daguerreotype was made in 1850. His third child, Rose, was born the following year.*

Sophia. "I need the sunshine of the children; even their little quarrels and naughtinesses would be a blessing to me. I need thee, above all. Come home! Come home!"

Unlike some husbands, he was not indifferent to the pressures upon Sophia in managing a household. "After a woman has become a mother," he said, "she may find rest in Heaven, but nowhere else." But Sophia didn't feel sorry for herself. She told her mother in 1848, "I am so happy that I require nothing more."

To port duties, writing, and family, Hawthorne added the responsibility of managing the Salem Lyceum. He handled signing on lecturers, arranging their housing, entertainment, publicity, fees. The roster of speakers he secured included his Concord friends—Emerson, Thoreau, and Alcott—plus such eminent men as Senator Daniel Webster, Senator Charles Sumner, and Horace Mann. For a man who shunned celebrity and wouldn't lecture himself, it was a strange thing to do.

Busy as he was, he did not neglect the local Democratic leaders, enjoying their company over a good cigar and a drink. With them he rode to Boston to see the fireworks display on July 4, 1848—Independence Day and his own forty-fourth birthday. A few months later, in November, the Whigs won the presidential election, elevating General Zachary Taylor, hero of the Mexican War, to the White House. It meant Hawthorne, like other Democratic jobholders, might be out of work. No matter which party was in power, the spoils system operated.

In June 1849, the expected axe fell. He put up a fight to retain his job, but even with the help of prominent supporters, he failed. Some thought his literary standing would save him; it didn't. That summer of 1849 was a sad one. He needed the surveyor's salary to live on, and he still had old debts to pay. Added to his anxiety was grief over the rapid decline of his mother's health. She died on July 31, 1849, leaving him more deeply shaken than he could imagine. Trying to cheer him up, Sophia suggested that he would now be able to write his book.

What book?

And where would they live?

The Scarlet Letter

THE BOOK Sophia said Hawthorne was free to write after he lost his job was *The Scarlet Letter*. The story had been growing in his mind many years before he began to work in the Custom House. An 1836 journal hints at a story of sin and shame. But he could not get it down on paper. His 1844 notebook reveals that he was haunted by the tale of a woman sentenced to walk the streets of Salem with a scarlet *A* on the breast of her gown as punishment for her sin in committing adultery. And in 1847, he had noted his intent to write a story about the effect of revenge on the person who indulges in it.

Now, after suffering two deep injuries—the loss of his livelihood and the loss of his mother—he stayed in his room day after day, writing "immensely" nine hours straight, Sophia said. She was "almost frightened about it. . . . He has become tender from confinement and brain work."

For six months, he held to that level of high tension until early in February 1850, when he came down to read the closing passage

Hawthorne (center) *with his publishers James T. Fields* (left) *and William Davis Ticknor* (right)

of the story to Sophia. "It broke her heart," Hawthorne told Bridge. "It is a hell-fired story." He feared it was too dark and forbidding for the general reader. To balance it, Hawthorne wanted to include in the same volume a group of his short stories.

Hearing that Hawthorne had been ill, James T. Fields, partner in the Boston publishing house of Ticknor & Fields he had become friendly with, came to Salem for a visit. Fields told him it was time to publish whatever he had been writing all these years in Salem. "Nonsense," Hawthorne replied. "Who would risk publishing a book for me, the most unpopular writer in America?"

"I would," said Fields.

"What madness!" Hawthorne exclaimed.

Fields insisted he must have been working on something.

"Nothing," was the reply.

Fields noticed a chest of drawers behind Hawthorne and wondered if some manuscript might not be hidden away there. "No, no," Hawthorne said, looking surprised, but shaking his head.

As Fields was hurrying down the stairs to catch his train back to Boston, Hawthorne came racing after him "with a roll of manuscript in his hands," saying, "How in heaven's name did you know this thing was there? . . . It is either very good or very bad—I don't know which."

On the train, Fields read what would become world renowned as *The Scarlet Letter*. He thought it superb. He convinced Hawthorne the story could stand alone, as a novel. Hawthorne had thought it should be just one story among several to be included in a single volume. Still uneasy, Hawthorne insisted on adding a long introduction about how the story came to be written. The fictional narrator, surveyor of the Salem Custom House, tells how he found in the attic of the Custom House a mysterious package containing a manuscript telling of the life of Hester Prynne in Puritan Boston two centuries earlier. Having lost his job, the narrator decided to become a literary man and tell the story of what happened in that Puritan town of colonial New England.

While awaiting publication of the novel, Sophia found a house for them in the country. It was on the Tappan estate in Lenox, a village of about 1,500 people in the Berkshire Hills of western Massachusetts. The little red farmhouse was offered the Hawthornes rent free by Caroline Tappan, an old friend of Sophia's who had married into a rich family of the region.

The Mystery of Sin

The mystery of sin. What is it? What does it mean? Does its mark pass down through the generations? Such questions were often in Hawthorne's mind. Many of his tales fix upon that theme. No wonder, when you recall the role of his ancestors in the persecution of the Quakers and in the Salem witch trials. From childhood on, he was fascinated and disturbed by the stories of his kinfolk.

The Scarlet Letter, his novel of some two hundred pages, takes place in seventeenth-century Boston, then a Puritan settlement. The Puritans were known for their fierce intolerance of dissenting ideas and behavior. Hawthorne tells a dark story of a single, forbidden act of passion that over a period of seven years changes the lives of a woman, her child, and two men in the community.

The story opens with a young woman, Hester Prynne, led from the town prison with the scarlet letter *A* on the breast of her clothing, and carrying her baby, Pearl, in her arms. The scarlet letter and her public shaming are punishment for her sin, and for her refusal to reveal the name of the man with whom she had an affair.

The other main characters are Roger Chillingsworth, her husband from the days they lived in England, and Arthur Dimmesdale, the town's young minister and secretly father of the child, Pearl.

Hester, the central figure, is a strong, independent character who struggles to maintain her self-respect in a community that scorns her. She manages to support herself and her child, and in the end, to win a place in that society.

The conflict between Puritan morality and human passion is not merely an underlying theme but the very basis of the plot in The Scarlet Letter, *considered by many to be Hawthorne's greatest work. This undated illustration shows Hester Prynne carrying her baby, Pearl, in her arms.*

The three main scenes of the novel take place at the town scaffold. The moods spin from emotional highs to suicidal despair. Delving more deeply than any American writer before him into the minds and hearts of his characters, Hawthorne created America's first psychological novel. It went beyond its Puritan framework to dramatize the impact of shame and guilt on conscience and character, a universal theme.

Hawthorne insisted on paying at least some rent, however. They agreed on $150 a year. The house had a good view of meadow, lake, Stockbridge Bowl, and Monument Mountain. Nearby were an orchard and spruce grove. There was a vegetable garden Hawthorne cultivated, and a barnyard to one side. They would stay for one winter and two summers.

Hawthorne had not been in the region for eleven years. In that time, it had become fashionable. Other writers now lived there or visited often. The poet Oliver Wendell Holmes, the novelist Catharine Sedgewick, and soon Herman Melville, working on his novel *Moby Dick*. Fanny Kemble, the English actress and author, had a home there too.

It would take money to move, money they didn't have. O'Sullivan came to their aid, sending $100 the *Democratic Review* owed Hawthorne and another $100 as an advance against future work. Still, it wasn't enough. Then came a letter from George Hillard. It contained the sum of $500 his old friend had collected from readers (probably including Hillard himself and Longfellow) who, he said, admired Hawthorne's stories and knew he needed help. They were only paying "in a very imperfect measure, the debt we owe you for what you have done for American literature. . . . Let no shadow of despondency, my dear friend, steal over you. Your friends do not and will not forget you." Reading this brought tears to Hawthorne's eyes.

Ticknor & Fields published the first edition of the novel in May 1850 at seventy-five cents per copy. The 2,500 copies sold quickly. By September, another 3,500 copies had been sold.

The firm was one of the most successful in America, drawing in the leading writers of Boston and Concord, among others. Fields, thirteen years younger than Hawthorne, was a shrewd, energetic, and sociable businessman who introduced modern methods of book promotion. He knew how to extract favorable notices from influential critics. Working with so shy an author as

Hawthorne, he was nevertheless able to commit him to new editions of earlier works as well as pledges for future writing.

Now Hawthorne could write Bridge that he had in sight the "only sensible ends" of the writing life: "First, the pleasurable toil of writing; second, the gratification of one's family and friends; and lastly, the solid cash."

Solid cash? It wasn't all that much. His royalties came to only $450. Still, it was much better than he'd done before.

Earning good reviews makes any writer feel great. Hawthorne read little but praise as reviews streamed in. "Extraordinary power. . . ." "Has mastered the whole philosophy of guilt. . . ." "So deep in thought and condensed in style. . . ." "A vigorous reach of imagination. . . ." "A splendor of portraiture. . . ." "Wonderful instinct and skill. . . ." Some reviewers, however, saw the subject of adultery as a scandalous choice for an author to make. And to apply such fine writing to that theme was "inappropriate."

In Salem a small tempest blew up over what "The Custom House" introduction had to say about some of the local political figures, the Whigs. Had Hawthorne shown more animosity than intended? "If I escape town without being tarred and feathered I shall consider it good luck," he said. Should he withdraw the offensive passages from the second edition? He considered it, but instead without changing a word, added that he meant no ill-feeling of any kind, personal or political. It only made Salemites angrier.

With *The Scarlet Letter* finished and published, Hawthorne was through forever with Salem. "Henceforth," he said, "it ceases to be a reality of my life. I am a citizen of somewhere else." That somewhere was the little red farmhouse in Lenox, Massachusetts.

In May 1850, the family moved into the red house. It was small, but snug, with five rooms on the first floor. Sophia converted the entry hall into a parlor with fireplace. Upstairs were four small rooms, including a study for Hawthorne. He planted lots of vegetables that summer, while the children spent almost all day outdoors, getting brown as berries.

Out of that small study came more literary work than at any other time in Hawthorne's life. In the next two years, he would write two more major novels—*The House of the Seven Gables* and *The Blithedale Romance,* plus a new edition of *Twice-Told Tales* and a reprinting of the earlier children's work, *True Stories from History and Biography.*

A New Friend, a New Novel

A FEW MONTHS after settling in at Lenox, Hawthorne met Herman Melville, who was visiting a cousin in the Berkshires. They were among a party of seven men and women setting out to picnic atop nearby Monument Mountain. Later that afternoon, they also visited the Ice Glen, which looked, Hawthorne said, "as if the Devil had torn his way through a rock and left it all jagged behind him."

That chance meeting began a friendship remarkable in literary history. Each had read and enjoyed the other's books. Hawthorne liked Melville so much that he asked him to spend a few days with him before returning home. The two men, Hawthorne, now forty-six, and Melville, thirty-one, had much in common, and they hit it off. Only two weeks after their meeting, the *Literary World* carried a passionate two-part review of Hawthorne's *Mosses from an Old Manse*. The review, unsigned and written before the men met, was by Melville. A review—four years after *Mosses* had been published! Melville, who had just read it for the first time, said that was

Melville (left), *pictured in 1847, and Hawthorne* (right), *pictured in 1851, held each other's writings in the highest regard. In fact, Melville would later dedicate his masterpiece,* Moby Dick, *to Hawthorne.*

because the book was only getting better and better all that while. He praised the great power of blackness in Hawthorne that fixes and fascinates the reader. And even he compared Hawthorne with Shakespeare for plunging so deeply into the universe.

Of course Hawthorne delighted in the review, but he said it praised him "more than I deserve." The editor of the *Literary Review* sent Hawthorne copies of three Melville novels: *Mardi, Redburn,* and *White-Jacket.* Hawthorne read them with increasing appreciation, commenting that "no writer ever put the reality before his reader more unflinchingly than he does. . . . *Mardi* is a rich book, with depths here and there that compel a man to swim for his life."

By the time Melville visited the Hawthornes for a few days early in September, Hawthorne knew he was the author of the review of *Mosses.* When Melville left, Sophia said she found him "a man with a true warm heart & a soul & an intellect—with life to his finger-tips." During the visit, Hawthorne continued writing *The House of the Seven Gables* in the mornings, while Melville went for walks.

Probably as a result of their warm, new friendship, Melville soon bought Arrowhead—a house on the outskirts of Pittsfield, several miles from the Hawthornes. And there he worked on writing *Moby Dick*.

In November Hawthorne wrote Fields that his new book, *The House of the Seven Gables*, was demanding "more care and thought" than *The Scarlet Letter*. It didn't go smoothly; good writing rarely does. He suffered doubts, hesitations, worries, fears. Sometimes, he said, "there are points where a writer gets bewildered, and cannot form any judgment of what he has done, nor tell what to do next. In these cases it is best to keep quiet."

The House of the Seven Gables in Salem inspired Hawthorne's novel of the same name.

The House of the Seven Gables

Hawthorne called *The House of the Seven Gables* a romance. Like so many of his works, it is a melding of realism and fantasy. Hawthorne's preface to the story tells us right off what its meaning is:

> The author has provided himself with a moral;—the truth namely, that the wrong-doing of one generation lives into the successive ones, and divesting itself of every temporary advantage, becomes a pure and uncontrollable mischief.

Hepzibah Pyncheon, the grumpy but lovable old woman who occupies the house of seven gables, is the descendant of a family under a curse laid upon them in colonial times by the laborer Matthew Maule, victim of a Pyncheon's greed.

The other major characters include Clifford Pyncheon, Hepzibah's brother, broken by three decades in prison on a false charge of murdering his uncle. The wealthy Judge Jaffrey Pyncheon, a cousin, is a respected figure in the small New England town, but beneath the smiling facade is a voracious appetite for wealth and more wealth. Then there is Holgrave, a young boarder in the attic, who is a daguerreotypist, Socialist, and, unknown to the others, a descendant of the Maules who invoked the curse long ago. Finally, there is Phoebe Pyncheon, seventeen as the story begins. She is the lovely young cousin of the Pyncheons whose charm, wisdom, and strength transform the others.

Although the plot is ingenious and the characters sometimes depicted in the manner of Dickens, the net effect is more like a painting than a novel rooted in reality. It is Hawthorne's use of language—his is a prose that glows and ignites the reader's feelings.

By late January 1851, Hawthorne was ready to read the new book to Sophia. Both thought it even better than *The Scarlet Letter*. But an author's opinion of his book, "just after completing it," he said, "is worth little or nothing; he being then in the hot or cold fit of a fever, and certain to rate it too high or too low." Two weeks later, he sent the manuscript to Fields, who published it quickly. To Bridge, Hawthorne wrote that the new book was better than *The Scarlet Letter* because it was "more characteristic of my mind, and more proper and natural for me to write."

Almost everyone has disagreed. It's considered to be his second-best book, more pleasant to write, perhaps, because it wasn't torn out of the depths of his heart and mind. As he himself said, the author is not always the best judge of his work. "Hawthorne was never to understand what he had done in *The Scarlet Letter*," Mark Van Doren believed.

Reviewers liked the new novel. One of them called it "sure of immediate popularity and permanent fame." A British critic said that Hawthorne's two novels ranked him "amongst the most original and complete novelists that have appeared in modern times."

On May 20, 1851, the Hawthornes' third and last child, Rose, was born. "A very promising child," Hawthorne wrote his sister Louisa, "kicking violently and crying most obstreperously."

Happy as Hawthorne was to have a new baby, it meant his economic worries increased. Even though, by modern standards, prices for necessities were low: milk, 3 cents a quart; butter, 14 cents a pound; eggs, 11 cents a dozen; veal, 6 cents a pound; beef, 9 cents a pound; wood, $3 a cord. So Sophia's records inform us.

Although what he called his "baby books" made little money, he decided now to reenter the field with *A Wonder Book for Girls and Boys*. It would be his most successful children's book. He had loved classical stories when he was a child, and now he drew upon those myths for his new book. He "modernized" them, he said, "so that they may be felt by children of these days. I shall purge out all the old heathen wickedness, and put in a moral wherever practicable."

The book is written "with affection and warmth, in a joyful, shimmering style," said his biographer, E. H. Miller. Excellent illustrations add to its quality. Translations also made it popular in Argentina, Chile, and Russia.

A Wonder Book was just off the press when Hawthorne began work on a follow-up book, *Tanglewood Tales for Girls and Boys*. It contains six myths, "done up in excellent style," he bragged, "purified from all moral stains, recreated as good as new, or better—and fully equal, in their way, to Mother Goose." His aim, he said, was to throw "the blessed sunshine" into the old legends often so "hideous, melancholy and miserable."

A quarrel with Mrs. Tappan led the Hawthornes to give up the farmhouse in Lenox. Hawthorne had come to dislike the Berkshire climate, complaining that it was either too cool or too warm. More likely he was feeling miserable about the unrelenting pressure to make enough money to take care of his family properly. Maybe a change of place would bring a change of luck? They began looking for a house.

When nothing suitable turned up, Sophia's sister, Mary Mann, suggested that temporarily they take the Manns' house in West Newton, near Boston, while newly elected Congressman Horace Mann and his family would be in Washington. The rent was high, $350, but soon they hoped to find a place to buy. Fields and his partner generously offered them an advance in money if necessary.

Utopia Revisited

IN NOVEMBER 1851, the Hawthornes moved into the Mann house in West Newton. Here he began to work on a new book, *The Blithedale Romance*, growing out of his experience at Brook Farm years ago. He had scarcely covered a sheet of paper when he came down with influenza. And the whole family, including the cook, got sick immediately after. The viral disease is powerful, and periodic epidemics have devastated whole populations. It turned their house into a virtual hospital for a while. Luckily, all survived, and Hawthorne got back to his writing.

Six months later, the book was finished. He sent the manuscript to a friend for an opinion, saying only Sophia had read it, but though she liked it, a wife's approval was not real criticism. Then he added, "if you should spy ever so many defects, I cannot promise to amend them; the metal hardens very soon after I pour it out of my melting pot into the mould."

Ticknor and Fields had no problem with it. They sent it to the printer promptly.

In *The Blithedale Romance,* Hawthorne invents a first-person narrator, Miles Coverdale. This may be because he wanted to work some of his own personal history into it. Melville too had done this in *Moby Dick.* But so have many other novelists.

The book clings more closely to the actual, rather than the allegorical he had used so often before. It offers Hawthorne's view of what happens when a small group of idealistic people try to create a Utopian community. Some have called it a cruel portrait of the conflict within social reformers—the clash between the ideals they profess and their actual practices. Confident in their own moral virtue, when given the authority, they control the lives of others to their own personal advantage.

Because Salemites had been angered by what they considered to be malign portraits of local people in *The House of the Seven Gables,* Hawthorne tried to forestall such criticism by claiming that the fictional characters in the new novel did not reflect in any way real persons.

He attempted to do this by sketching the four major characters: "The self-concentrated philanthropist; the high-spirited Woman, bruising herself against the narrow limitations of her sex; the weakly Maiden, whose tremulous nerves endow her with Sibylline attributes; the minor Poet, beginning life with strenuous aspirations which die out with youthful fervor—all these might have been looked for at Brook Farm, but, by some accident, never made their appearance there."

This disclaimer suggests he knew quite well that the characters were but thinly disguised portraits of real people he met at Brook Farm, and elsewhere too.

During the summer of 1852, the publisher issued two printings of the novel, totaling some 7,500 copies. A fair beginning, but sales fell off rapidly. The reviews were lukewarm. One reviewer said the suicide of Zenobia, a leading character, was "shocking and unnecessary." Another complained that

Hawthorne was too harsh on reformers. Some reviewers went the IO5 opposite way, holding the author was too tender on the dreamers of social reform.

In London, Fields managed to sell rights to the book to an English publisher. Returning home, however, he too was let down by the poor sales, blaming it on the story's grim tone. He hoped there would be "no more Blithedales," please!

In May the Hawthornes resettled in Concord. They bought Bronson Alcott's house, long up for sale, paying $1,500 for it, together with 9 acres (almost 4 hectares). A few months later they bought 8 more acres across the road for $500. The house, old and

The Hawthornes purchased their Concord home from prominent Transcendentalist and educator Bronson Alcott, father of Louisa May Alcott, who would later gain fame for her novels Little Women *and* Little Men. *Here a group of women are shown gathered round the fireplace in the Alcott home before the sale to the Hawthornes in 1852.*

rundown, had been added to haphazardly by Alcott. Hawthorne named it the Wayside because it sat so close to the road.

After many years of renting houses, this was the first one the Hawthornes owned. The family was happy there. Hawthorne explored the woods and fields with the children: Una, now eight, Julian six, and Rose going on two. One winter day, they built a snowman up so high that it lasted until the spring.

With the Emersons and other neighbors, they enjoyed picnics outdoors. And Sophia gave her own and several other children lessons in reading, geography, drawing, and the Bible. A little later, Hawthorne's son Julian would attend the school of a recent Concord settler, Frank Sanborn. In the same classes were Emerson's son, two sons of the abolitionist John Brown, and the sons of Horace Mann.

Concord was close enough to Boston and Salem for them to see their old friends there. Fields would come to visit and Ticknor sent Hawthorne cigars and wines.

That summer of 1852, national attention focused on the political conventions, with the Whigs and Democrats choosing candidates for the 1852 presidential election. The Democrats picked Franklin Pierce, the college friend of Hawthorne, as their candidate. A shrewd politician, Pierce had been careful as U.S. senator from New Hampshire not to offend the Southern Democrats. Which meant pussyfooting around the explosive issue of slavery.

The political pot was coming to a boil in the 1850s. The western lands were filling up with people from all parts of the East and South, we well as immigrants from abroad. Which way would the new states go? Would they add to the political strength of the slaveholders? Or to the opponents who wanted to see slavery ended nationally?

With the Compromise of 1850, adopted by Congress in September, the new territories wrested from Mexico would decide the slavery question for themselves. The slave trade would be outlawed, but not slavery in the District of Columbia. A new and

Hawthorne's friend and former Bowdoin classmate Franklin Pierce was the Democratic nominee for U.S. president in 1852. Hawthorne wrote a political biography of Pierce, but his backing of the pro-slavery candidate angered many of his abolitionist friends.

harsher fugitive slave law would force the North to return runaways to their owners.

At the news of his old friend's nomination, Hawthorne seized the opportunity to advance his classmate's political career by offering to write his campaign biography. Pierce had not been a front-runner for the nomination. It had taken forty-nine ballots before he came out on top. His name and his achievements (very few) needed to be promoted to the country.

Pierce promptly said, yes, you're the right man. Hawthorne asked Ticknor if the partners would publish it. It should be a good book because he and Pierce had been such close friends since college days. And, he added, "I seek nothing from him."

Who believed that? Wouldn't anyone helping to elect a president this way expect a political plum in return? A well-paid diplomatic post, for instance?

Hawthorne's sister Louisa didn't like that talk. Politics to her was a dirty business, and Pierce was pro-slavery. Away in Saratoga Springs, New York, at the time, she decided to visit Concord, going by steamboat down the Hudson River to New York City, and then by land up to Concord. On July 20, her steamboat, the *Henry Clay*, began to race with another ship, the *Armenia*, when suddenly something went horribly wrong. The two boats collided, and fire raced through the *Clay*. There being no lifeboats, passengers leaped into the river, hoping to swim to shore. Louisa was among those who never made it.

News of her death was a terrible shock. At first, Hawthorne couldn't go on with the Pierce book. Then, hardening himself, he urged Ticknor to publicize the book in advance. "We are politicians now; and you must not expect to conduct yourself like a gentlemanly publisher." He himself set about gathering material for the book through interviews and documentary research.

Introducing the biography, a short one, Hawthorne asserted he himself was not a politician, only a citizen concerned with the welfare of his country. Pierce, he wrote, may not be a great man, or a great orator, but he is a man of great heart, steady and generous. The country needs such a leader. Well, said Horace Mann, "If he makes out Pierce to be a great man or a brave man, it will be the greatest work of fiction he ever wrote."

Not surprisingly, the reviews of *The Life of Franklin Pierce* were pro—when the publication was Democratic, and anti—when it was Whig. While Hawthorne's aim was to display Pierce as the best candidate, the *New York Times* concluded that the book showed up Pierce as an awful choice.

Meanwhile, Hawthorne joined Pierce in Maine for the fiftieth-anniversary celebration of Bowdoin College. Friends now for thirty years, there was the strongest bond of affection between them.

Hawthorne knew that among friends in Boston and Concord, his service to Pierce would be viewed as detestable. Horace and Mary Mann raged; how could he back such a pro-slavery man? And how could he blind himself to the misery of enslaved millions in the hope of personal advancement?

Well, he could, and he did.

What especially angered abolitionists was a passage in the biography where Hawthorne says Pierce "considered that the evil of abolition would be certain, while this good [emancipation] was, at best, a contingency." Adding that if the slaves were freed, it would bring about "the ruin of two races which now dwelt together in greater peace and affection, it is not too much to say, than had ever elsewhere existed between the taskmaster and the serf." Or to put it bluntly, he was saying that the slaves were happy, and freedom would be bad for them.

Pierce supported all parts of the Compromise of 1850 as being necessary. The Founding Fathers, he argued, had not ended slavery when adopting the Constitution. And since the Fugitive Slave Law was now the law of the land, everyone must obey it.

Would they? "This filthy enactment was made in the 19th century, by people who could read and write," wrote Emerson in his journal. "I will not obey it, by God." Nor did the Concord abolitionists mean to obey it.

In a letter to a Salem friend, the conservative Democrat Zachariah Burchmore, Hawthorne said, "I have not, as you suggest, the slightest sympathy for the slaves; or, at least, not half so much as for the laboring whites, who, I believe, are ten times worse off than the Southern negroes."

Hawthorne was a victim of the old curse of white superiority. Like most Americans then, including the artists, the intellectuals, and even some abolitionists, he considered blacks to be an inferior people. In that time, it was a common belief that African Americans were only fit to be slaves. The prejudiced ones did not know (nor do most people today know) that people of all colors—white, yellow, brown, red, black—have been enslaved, and have themselves enslaved others. One wonders if Hawthorne had read a powerful indictment of racism published twenty years earlier, would his views have been changed? The book, written by

Lydia Maria Child of Massachusetts, was *An Appeal in Favor of That Class of Americans Called Africans*. (Published in 1833, the classic is still in print.)

On Saturday morning, February 15, 1851, Shadrach, an escaped Virginia slave working as a waiter in Boston, was the first black to be seized by a federal marshal under the new law. Early that afternoon, two blacks rescued the runaway from the courthouse where he was held and rushed him out of town. At three o'clock on Sunday afternoon, a carriage with drawn blinds pulled up in Concord, and Shadrach was put in the capable hands of Francis Bigelow, the town blacksmith, who sent him on to the next station, toward Canada and freedom. Concord had long been an antislavery center and was a stop on the Underground Railroad. The Emersons, the Alcotts, and the Thoreaus had special rooms in their houses to shelter fugitive slaves.

Hardly six months later, Hawthorne's friend Thoreau defied the fugitive slave law. A slave who had escaped from his master in Virginia had been forwarded by the Underground Railroad to Concord. He stayed overnight at the Thoreau home before being helped on toward Canada. A year later, when another runaway had been taken in for overnight shelter by Thoreau, a friend, Moncure Conway, happened to be visiting. He recorded Thoreau's "singularly tender devotion" to the fugitive, feeding him, bathing his swollen feet, making him feel at home, and assuring him he need "have no fear that any power should again wrong him."

Thoreau was one of many who acted not only secretly to help the fugitive slaves but publicly to protest against the Fugitive Slave Law. On the Fourth of July, 1854 (Hawthorne's fiftieth birthday), Thoreau gave a powerful speech in Framingham, Massachusetts, at the annual meeting of the antislavery society. In it he attacked both press and church as defenders of slavery and appealed for a higher standard of morality.

"The law," he said, "will never make men free; it is men who have got to make the law free. They are the lovers of law and order who observe the law when the government breaks it."

On November 2, 1852, Franklin Pierce was elected the fourteenth president of the United States. He took office on March 4, 1853.

On March 26, the president's nomination of Nathaniel Hawthorne as U.S. consul in Liverpool, England, was approved by the Senate. It was the post Hawthorne had set his hopes on. For to be the consul in Liverpool, one of the world's busiest ports, meant you were assured of large fees. It was said that the post brought in $30,000 to $40,000 a year—a huge sum for that era.

Shortly after Pierce heard confirmation of his presidential election in November 1852, he hired portraitist George P. A. Healy to paint his likeness. At the same time, Pierce asked Healy to piant a likeness of the president-elect's campaign biographer and longtime friend, Nathaniel Hawthorne (left).

Our Man in Liverpool

NO SOONER was Hawthorne's appointment made public than people hoping for a government job began pestering him to use his influence on their behalf. His experience had made him cynical enough to advise the hopefuls "to conceal any deficiencies (moral, intellectual or educational, whatever else)." Just get the appointment in whatever way. The business is to establish yourself, somehow, anywhere.

He tried hard to help Herman Melville, especially. For he too badly needed a steady income. But nothing came of it. Not even Melville's father-in-law, Lemuel Shaw, chief justice of the Massachusetts Supreme Court, was able to swing an appointment for the author.

Two days after Hawthorne turned forty-nine, on July 6, 1853, his family boarded the *Niagara*, a Cunard steamship bound for Liverpool. With them on the eleven-day voyage was Hawthorne's publisher William Ticknor. Before they left, Hawthorne had had a private meeting in Washington with President Pierce. At Pierce's request, he stayed in the capitol longer than planned, treated as a literary celebrity, which according to Ticknor, annoyed him very much.

While they would be gone in England, the Wayside house was taken over by Sophia's father, Dr. Peabody, and the family of one of his sons. (Sophia's mother, after a brief illness, had died in January.) In Liverpool they settled into a furnished house, paying a rental of $800 a year.

They would be spending six years abroad. Four of them in England, and then two on the Continent. Hawthorne would do his work faithfully at the consulate. He hoped not only to support his family well now, but to save enough money so that, added to his books' royalties, his family would be secure even after he died. And then there was the desire to gather the material

While Hawthorne carried out his appointment as consul to England, the family lived in this house in Rock Ferry, outside of Liverpool, England.

and insights that his imagination might transform into new and maybe even better works of fiction.

On August 1, he took over his consular office on the Liverpool docks. It had two rooms, one for him and the other for his clerk and the vice-consul, both experienced Englishmen. They took care of the routine chores. To the port, one of the world's busiest, came such American products as cotton and sugarcane. And to his door came "the most rascally set of sailors that ever were seen—dirty, desperate, and altogether pirate-like in aspect." They were looking for help of all kinds. In his notebook, Hawthorne spelled out the multiple duties expected of him as the highest-ranking American official:

> The duties of the office carried me to prisons, police-courts, hospitals, lunatic asylums, coroner's inquests, death-beds, funerals, and brought me in contact with insane people, criminals, ruined speculators, wild adventurers, diploma-tists, brother-consuls, and all manner of simpletons and unfortunates, in greater number and variety than I had ever dreamed of as pertaining to America; in addition to whom there was an equivalent multitude of English rogues, dex-terously counterfeiting the genuine Yankee article.

Besieged for assistance and advice, he shrank from the necessity of giving it. It was in his nature to believe there were "about as many reasons for acting in one way as in any other, and quite as many for acting in neither."

From Hawthorne's journal we learn of the hellish life of merchant seamen. Flogged, mutilated, even in danger of being murdered by sadistic or terrified captains and mates, they brought their grievances to the consul's office when their ships entered port. He could do little but see that the men were released from service and their wages paid. Often brutal captains unfairly discharged crewmen and refused to pay their wages.

When Hawthorne's reports to Washington of such miseries brought no results, he wrote Senator Charles Sumner, urging that he campaign for remedial legislation. But to no avail. Nothing changed.

The consul's job provided no regular salary. The shipping determined his income. Each time he signed a consular receipt for a ship's merchandise he was paid $2. The income varied from day to day. Sometimes it could add up to $250 in a single day. His mood varied with the day's receipts. In one two-month period it totaled $3,400; he was ecstatic. He wrote Ticknor to invest it for him, adding, "If I can once see $20,000 in a pile I shan't care much for being turned out of office."

As a man with a literary reputation on both sides of the Atlantic, Hawthorne would have been welcomed by England's writers. But he made no effort to reach out to eminent authors like Dickens, Thackeray, Tennyson, or George Eliot. He did meet some poets, explorers, actors, and politicians at the frequent breakfasts hosted by the poet and literary patron Richard Milnes, who would later become instrumental in making Emerson known in Britain.

His standing as both author and consul brought him numerous invitations to public functions that he found "irksome beyond expression." At civic banquets, he sometimes was called upon to make a speech which he did "prettily" after "gulping down champagne which is best adapted to bringing out my heroic qualities," he said.

His observations weren't limited to the upper-class English. As when at home, he liked to walk the mean streets, to record in his notebook the life of people at the other end of society. His prejudices are plain in the notebooks, especially his anti-Semitism.

When the Crimean War ended with the English celebrating their victory over the Russians, he and Julian watched the jubilant crowds in the streets. He praised the English for being so solidly behind their government, contrasting them to Americans who were ashamed of their government during the Mexican War.

Hawthorne (far right) *and Sophia* (far left) *on an outing in Oxford, England, in 1856*

He filled his notebooks so regularly and so fully that it would seem it was a substitute for his failure to write any fiction during these years. Sophia wrote her sister that with her husband working eight hours a day at his office "he could no more write a syllable than he could build a cathedral."

The critical and unvarnished honesty with which he set down his views of English life, if published, would "bring a terrible hornet's nest about my ears," he told Ticknor. (His English journal, more than 300,000 words, was not published until 1941.)

Despite the wearying burden of his duties, he found time in the evenings to read aloud to the children. If it wasn't *Robinson Crusoe*, then it was a story he made up on the spot. He played all sorts of games with them. When Julian took fencing lessons, his father picked up the foil and clowned wildly with it.

To her father and sisters back in Concord, Sophia sent long letters that reflect her acute awareness of the gulf between classes in

His family often passed the time listening to Hawthorne read aloud or tell stories, as depicted in this undated illustration.

England: "It is all stereotyped, crystallized, with the repose and quiet in it of an immovable condition of caste." She wrote of "the brutal misery" in which the lowest orders are plunged. Observing this made it seem as if "everything must be turned upside down rather than for one moment more to tolerate such suffering, such bestiality."

Never in robust health, Sophia fell victim to the raw, damp climate of Liverpool's winters. In the fall of 1854, after her father died, her racking cough worsened. A doctor urged that she leave England for a better climate in the coming winter. Their friend John O'Sullivan was now U.S. minister to Portugal, and with his encouragement, in October Hawthorne sent Sophia and the two girls to sunny Lisbon. Julian remained with his father.

During the eight months Sophia and the girls were gone, Hawthorne kept busy as usual at the consulate. But in after hours, he confided to his notebook, he "suffered woefully from low spirits. I sleep ill, lying awake late at night to think sad thoughts. . . .

Nothing gives me any joy. I have learned what the bitterness of exile is. . . . Life seems so purposeless as not to be worth the trouble of carrying it on any further."

In that sour mood, he wrote his friend Bridge that it sickened him to look back to America. He hated to hear of "the continual fuss and tumult and excitement and bad blood which we keep up about political topics. . . . We are the most miserable people on earth." And to Ticknor he wrote, "The United States are fit for many excellent purposes, but they are certainly not fit to live in." He sometimes thought of himself as an Englishman. Hadn't his first American ancestor left England in 1630? And here this Hawthorne was, home again after 223 years away.

From Lisbon, Sophia reported her health had improved and she was enjoying an exciting round of social and cultural life. The O'Sullivans escorted her often to the ballet and the opera, and she was invited to meet elegant people right up to the new, young king, Pedro V.

Alone in Liverpool, adding to Hawthorne's misery was the political news from home. Out in the Kansas territory, pro- and antislavery factions were fighting a bloody war for control of the legislature, with Pierce favoring the slavery faction. In May 1856, the abolitionist senator Charles Sumner was brutally beaten in the Senate chamber by a fanatical Southern congressman. During the summer, the Democrats passed over President Pierce and nominated James Buchanan in his place as their presidential candidate. And he would win the election. Few people disagreed that Pierce as president had been a disaster. Yet Hawthorne loved the man, seeing in him qualities almost no one else saw.

That November, on his way to the Mediterranean and Constantinople, Melville stopped in Liverpool to visit with Hawthorne. They spent several days together. Not having seen each other for years, it took a while to revive their old, warm connection. Hawthorne realized anew what a remarkable man his

friend was, noting in his journal that Melville has "a very high and noble nature, and better worth immortality than most of us."

Knowing that when Pierce left office his successor would appoint one of his own followers to the consulate, Hawthorne in February gave Buchanan notice that he would quit the consulate on August 31, 1857.

In his remaining six months on the job, Hawthorne kept pressing for measures to end the terrible state of the merchant marine, with all its crime and cruelties. The Buchanan administration denied that anything was wrong with the marine laws. They saw no problem with things as they were.

That spring and summer, Hawthorne and Sophia often went sightseeing in England and Scotland. Sophia too kept a notebook on their travels. Hawthorne wrote Ticknor that she "altogether excels me as a writer of travels. Her descriptions are the most perfect pictures that ever were put on paper; it is a pity they cannot be published; but neither she nor I would like to see her name on your list of female authors."

Several times he wailed about women daring to take on a man's profession, especially writing. "All women, as authors, are feeble and tiresome," he said. "I wish they were forbidden to write, on having their faces deeply scarified with an oyster shell." It was a false liberalism, he thought, to let women "add a girlish feebleness to the tottering infancy of our literature."

How did he take the enormous success of Harriet Beecher Stowe's antislavery novel, *Uncle Tom's Cabin*? Published in 1852, the same year his own *Blithedale Romance* appeared, it had sold 300,000 copies. Hawthorne's novel had sold 7,000 copies

It almost drove him crazy: "America is now wholly given over to a d_____d mob of scribbling women, and I should have no chance of success while the public taste is occupied with their trash—and should be ashamed of myself if I did succeed."

After four years at the consul's desk he was weary of the task. "I have received, and been civil to, at least 10,000 visitors since I came to England," he wrote Ticknor, "and I never wish to be civil to anybody again."

He was joking, at least in part. When he added up the financial results of his years at the consulate, the sum was quite positive. It had provided an income much greater than he had ever earned by writing. He had paid back the money Hillard and other friends had given him when he lost the Salem Custom House job. And he had sent funds to relieve two friends—Bridge and O'Sullivan—from their money troubles. Finally, the savings piled up in Liverpool would ensure the security of his family.

They had to put off leaving for the Continent because of a delay in the arrival of his replacement at the consulate. By the time the family left England, early in January 1858, Hawthorne was denouncing Liverpool as a black and miserable hole.

Maybe he would be happier in Italy?

The Marble Faun

THEY PASSED THROUGH France slowly, stopping briefly in one city after another, and two weeks later, on January 20, they reached Rome. With them was Ada Shepard, a young graduate of Antioch College who had agreed to work, only for her expenses, as the children's governess. With them also was Maria Mitchell, the American astronomer they'd met in Liverpool. She was famous for having discovered a new comet in 1847. She spent time with the Hawthornes in Rome, finding Hawthorne to be "a sad man. I could never tell why." She observed too that "Mrs. Hawthorne almost worshipped him."

Before leaving America, they had planned to spend a year in Italy. More because Sophia had longed to see "the cradle of the arts." Hawthorne too was glad to go, partly because it was cheaper to live there, and because he thought he would write again while seeing the sights.

That first spring in Rome, they entered the circle of Americans who had created an artists' colony away from home. Like

121

Hawthorne in his romances, the painters and sculptors excelled in allegories, expressing despair and triumph, victory and defeat. At the center of the colony was William Wetmore Story, the son of Supreme Court Justice Joseph Story. Writing poetry when young, he then studied law but ran off to Europe to settle in Rome. Among his fellow artists, he found a refuge from an America marching into the modern industrial age. In Rome, Story said, "all things are easy and careless in the out-of-doors life of the common people—all poses unsought, all groupings accidental, all action unaffected and unconscious. One meets nature at every turn—not braced up in prim forms, not conscious in manners, not made up into the fashionable or the proper, but impulsive, free and simple."

In Florence a group of American sculptors had found a home. Among them were Horatio Greenough, Thomas Crawford, and

American sculptor William Wetmore Story, who lived in Rome, sculpted this marble statue, entitled The Libyan Sibyl, *in 1868. Rome's rich history in arts and literature inspired many American artists, including Hawthorne.*

Hiram Powers. Like many of their generation, they had been raised on the Greek myths. Hawthorne's *Wonder Book* and *Tanglewood Tales* were the literary outcome of that education. So was Lydia Maria Child's *Philothea*, her novel of Greece in the time of Plato and Pericles.

In Rome the Americans met at cafés, strolled in the Coliseum in the moonlight, lingered at the Trevi Fountain, picnicked on the Appian Way. Evenings, they might gather at the apartment of Charlotte Cushman, the famous American actress who often wintered in Rome. This was the Italy the Hawthornes came to know, where they made new friends, absorbed new ideas, tasted the fresh flavors of a life so different from Salem or Concord or Liverpool.

The sculptor Story, whom Hawthorne first met in Salem, had made Italy his permanent home. A man of many talents—he could act, sing, sketch, write—he lived in the Palazzo Barberini, where the Hawthornes and their children could enjoy hearing such people as Robert Browning read from *The Pied Piper* and *The Ugly Duckling*.

During their long stay abroad, the children were tutored by young Ada Shepard. The depth of her knowledge and variety of her skills were a tribute to Horace Mann's Antioch College. She was fluent in French, Italian, and German, and acted as interpreter for the family. She gave Una, Julian, and Rose lessons in reading, writing, composition, Latin, Greek, arithmetic, algebra, geometry, geography, and history. Sometimes the children of other Americans joined her classes.

Writing to her boyfriend, Clay Badger, in America, she said she was living in "the happiest home-circle I have ever seen." After the first few months, she told Clay, "I love Mr. Hawthorne very much, and do not understand why people find him cold. He is certainly extremely reserved, but he is noble and true and good, and is full of kindly feeling. . . . His nature is like thine in many respects, dearest Clay"—which must have pleased her fiancé. As for her impression of Sophia: "I think he [Hawthorne] is ten times the man he might

Faun, *by Greek sculptor Praxiteles, is on display in the Vatican Museum in Rome. The work influenced Hawthorne's final novel,* The Marble Faun.

have been without her. . . . She is able to sympathize with him in his highest aspirations and is his companion in every mood."

It took Hawthorne a while to thaw out and let Rome warm his heart. He enjoyed watching Story sculpting his famous *Cleopatra,* but never let the artist know how much he liked it. He roamed the museums with Sophia, wondering about the mystery of art. What made this painting or that sculpture great? Why? How? Was it for everyone? Or just a few?

All the while, he was absorbing material he would work into his next—and last completed—novel, *The Marble Faun.* Its title refers to a work by the famous Greek sculptor, Praxiteles, who lived in the fourth century B.C. He made several statues of young satyrs, "creatures standing between humans and animals." The one Hawthorne had seen in Rome became his marble faun, given the title and character of Donatello. In 1858 he wrote in his notebook, "It seems to me that a story, with all sorts of fun and pathos in it, might be contrived on the idea of the faun's species having become intermingled with the human race. . . . The moral instincts and intellectual characteristics of the faun might be most picturesquely brought out, without detriment to the human interest of the story."

Two young women artists Hawthorne got to know in Italy fascinated him. Both sculptors, they were different from prim New Englanders he had known back home. He liked not only the work they did but the way they lived. One was Harriet Hosmer, of Watertown, Massachusetts. His notebook describes her:

> She had on petticoats, I think; but I did not look so low, my attention being chiefly drawn to a sort of man's sack of purple or plum-colored broadcloth, into the side-pockets of which her hands were thrust as she came forward to greet us. She withdrew one hand, however, and presented it cordially to my wife (whom she already knew) and to myself

American artist Harriet Hosmer, with her non-traditional style of dress and her independent, forward nature, made quite an impression on Hawthorne when they met while in Rome.

without waiting for an introduction. She had on a male shirt, collar, and cravat, with a brooch of Etruscan gold; and on her head was a picturesque little cap of black velvet. . . . There never was anything so jaunty as her movement and action; she was indeed very queer, but she seemed to be her actual self, and nothing affected or made up; so that, for my part, I give her full leave to wear what maysuit her best, and to behave as her inner woman prompts.

The other sculptor was Maria Louisa Lander, who came from his hometown, Salem. He noted, wonderingly, that she was

A young woman, living in almost perfect independence, thousands of miles from her New England home, going fearlessly about these mysterious streets, by night as well as by day, with no household ties, no rule or law but that within her; yet acting with quietness and simplicity and keeping, after all, within a homely line of right. Miss Lander has become strongly attached to Rome, and says that, when she dreams of home, it is merely of paying a short visit, and coming back before her trunk is unpacked.

Their personalities were so striking that elements of them are seen in the characterization of Hilda in *The Marble Faun*. It was said that many young American women who read the novel were drawn by it to Rome.

The Hawthornes spent several months in Florence, visiting studios, talking to artists. Hawthorne was very happy there. He wrote, "Really, if I could take root anywhere, I know not but it could as well be here as in another place. It would only be a kind of despair, however, that would ever make me dream of finding a home in Italy; a sense that I had lost my country through absence or incongruity, and that earth is not an abiding place."

Italy in Revolt

During his time in Italy, Hawthorne made few connections with Italians. His friends were other Americans living abroad. There is little indication in his letters or notebooks that he responded to the great upheaval in Italian life. The democratic-revolutionary Roman republic of 1848 had been suppressed by French invasion in 1849, followed by Garibaldi's leadership (1859–1860) of the struggle for the national unification of Italy.

Other Americans living in Italy, like Margaret Fuller, had given their emotional and political support to the revolutionary movement. But Hawthorne was not like her, or like Samuel Gridley Howe, the Boston doctor who had spent six years in Greece helping in its struggle to break free of Turkish domination. No, Hawthorne's interest in Italy was its works of art and the history of that art.

His experience abroad came early in the rising wave of American tourism. Gradually a thousand Americans yearly and then tens of thousands would make the grand tour of Europe. These were, of course, that class of people with the free time and money for travel. Among them, the wealthiest began to acquire European art for their own homes and for American museums.

Giuseppe Garibaldi became a national hero in Italy after driving out the country's foreign rulers.

Hawthorne in 1860 (top left), *Sophia in 1861* (top right), *and at left,* Una (left), Julian (center), *and* Rose (right) *in 1861. Both Una and Sophia were in poor health at this time, Una still weak from the malaria and typhus she had contracted in Italy, and Sophia recovering from the strain of caring for her critically ill daughter.*

In Florence he began writing his first draft of *The Marble Faun*. When they returned to Rome for the winter months he went on with the novel, hoping to complete it before returning to America. But in the fall, Una, now twelve, came down with malaria, a terrifying illness, and almost died. For months her father was so distraught he could not write a word in his journal. She recovered very slowly, but was never again fully healthy.

A few days later, a surprise visitor showed up. It was Franklin Pierce. The two old friends had not seen each other for six years and were delighted to be together again. Hawthorne was saddened to see the marks of wear and coming age in the former president. Pierce said he would never want to be in the White House again, yet he had enjoyed it while he was there. How could he not know what a miserable job the public thought he had done?

Arriving as Una was still struggling to recover, Pierce's sympathy was the deepest. He knew what the loss of a child meant, for he and his wife had lost three in early childhood. He has "so large and kindly a heart," wrote Hawthorne, and is "so tender and so strong," that he would always love him. He knew "each would do his best for the other as friend for friend."

The Hawthornes had planned to sail back to America in July 1859. But because of the laws governing copyright, in both England and the United States, they moved to England where they stayed for another year as Hawthorne finished the third draft of the novel. *The Marble Faun* was completed late in 1859 and published in 1860 in both countries almost simultaneously to prevent piracy of his work.

Now fifty-five, Hawthorne felt as uncertain about the worth of his book as he had when only a beginner in fiction. He told Fields that he wished that he were rich so he would never have to publish another book again, but only write for his own amusement.

When the book appeared, it drew mixed notices. "A master-piece," one reviewer said. Another thought the character Hilda "the loveliest type of American womanhood." Emerson called it "mush." In England Longfellow said it was "a wonderful book: but with the old dull pain that runs through all Hawthorne's writings." In England three editions were run up within the first month. In Germany a popular illustrated edition was published. The book was so crammed with details of places and things to see that tourists used it as a guidebook.

What bothered readers and reviewers most was the vagueness of the characterizations and of the book's ending. It showed "a want of finish" and left too many questions unanswered. What happened to the chief characters? The fault, if it be one, was deliberate. As Hawthorne pointed out in the novel's last chapter, "the actual experience of even the most ordinary life is full of events that never explain themselves either as regards their origin or their tendency."

In the summer of 1860, the Hawthornes resettled themselves in Concord. Not long before boarding the steamer, Hawthorne wrote Fields, "As regards going home, I alternate between a longing and a dread . . . I fear I have lost the capacity of living continually in any one place."

Concord— and Civil War

THAT FIRST SUMMER back in Concord was chaotic. After seven years away, the children were almost twice as big as before. The whole family felt it needed more room. Carpenters were hired to build a new wing to the Wayside. It included a tower room for the author's study, three stories high and twenty feet square. Underneath the roof it proved to be too hot in the summer and too hot as well in the winter because of the wood-burning stove.

The new wing cost Hawthorne $2,000, more than he had planned. He had to ask Ticknor to send $550, admitting he had turned a simple old farmhouse into an absurd mess. "If it would only burn down! But I have no such luck."

He had come home to an America on the eve of Civil War. While in England he had read the news of the raid on the federal arsenal at Harpers Ferry by John Brown and twenty-one followers in October 1859. Their aim was to liberate and arm slaves to strike against slavery in the heart of the South. But the raid failed when

Hawthorne's study, where he wrote The Life of Franklin Pierce *and finished* Tanglewood Tales *was in the tower. He deliberately had his desk facing toward the bookcases so that he would not be distracted by the beautiful view from the south-facing window.*

U.S. troops captured or killed his men, wounding Brown himself. After a quick trial, Brown was sentenced to death by hanging.

On December 2, the day of execution, a meeting was held in Concord, planned by Emerson, Thoreau, and Alcott. Emerson said Brown's "martyrdom . . . will make the gallow as glorious as the cross." And Thoreau declared, "He is not Old Brown any longer; he is an Angel of Light." Hawthorne (in England at the time), though he admired Brown's integrity, said, "Nobody was ever more justly hanged."

He meant that Brown and the abolitionists had miscalculated the possibilities. Maybe America needed change. But who could bring it about? It was in people's nature to be sinful. Didn't life prove that the Puritans were right to hold that evil is a reality in the world?

Reformers, progressives, radicals like John Brown underestimated virtue's weakness in its struggle with evil. Sophia wrote to a friend,

> I was glad to find that you believe that GOD'S Law would without wail have removed slavery, without this dreadful convulsive action. It always seems to me that Man is very arrogant in taking such violent measures to help GOD, who needs no help. I find no one in Concord—or hardly in Boston to whom I can utter such sentiments without exciting fiery indignation—My sisters cannot hear me speak a word— To my husband only I can speak. He is very all sided and can look serenely on opposing forces and do justice to each.

With the execution of Brown, the political parties became more fiercely partisan than ever. When Lincoln was elected, seven Southern slaveholding states seceded before Lincoln's inauguration in March 1861. "I go for the dissolution of the Union," Hawthorne told Ticknor. "If I could but be deprived of my political rights and left to my individual freedom," he would be content.

Sophia's sisters—Mary and Elizabeth—pitched into the heart of the antislavery cause. Elizabeth had gone down to Virginia to plead with the governor—without success—for the release of one of John Brown's men. When she tried to recruit young Una to the cause, Sophia objected, telling her sister to quit agitating the child. Sophia did not approve of Elizabeth's belief in Thoreau's doctrine of nonviolent resistance to unjust laws. She considered it dangerous and demoralizing.

Next-door-neighbor Louisa May Alcott, twenty-seven and a fledgling author, made up her own mind. Like her father, she was full of reverence and admiration for Old John Brown. She only regretted that she had not been born a man in this time of crisis. (Later she would serve as nurse to wounded Union soldiers in Washington's hospitals.)

Hawthorne found the political turmoil too much to take. His life became more solitary. Rather than face fierce arguments in Concord, he conveyed his feelings to friends in England. To one he wrote, "I am almost ashamed to say how little I care about the matter. . . . As to the South, I never loved it. We do not belong together; the Union is unnatural; a scheme of man, not an ordinance of God."

In the fall of 1860, the Hawthornes placed Julian, now fourteen, in the school run by Franklin Sanborn. He was a progressive educator as well as a bold abolitionist. But they would not enroll Una or Rose in the school. Sophia strongly opposed mixing boys and girls in the same classrooms.

That fall, Una again fell sick, her malaria returning, with frightening symptoms of mental illness as well.

Although Hawthorne seldom left his hillside home, he did rejoin the Saturday Club in Boston. It met once a month for dinner at the Parker House. Its members now included such notables as Longfellow, Emerson, Oliver Wendell Holmes, and Senator Charles Sumner. Hawthorne found it "an excellent institution with the privilege of first-rate society, and no duties but to eat one's dinners." He was so quiet at the dinners he seemed to one tablemate to be "like some pathetic Concord owl, brought into daylight and expected to wink and be lively in company." Another noted that he buried his eyes in his plate as though daring anyone to ask him a question.

When the South's bombardment of Fort Sumter in April 1861 began the Civil War, Hawthorne was surprised to find it shook him out of his dismal spirits. He told his friend Bridge that he "couldn't quite understand what we are fighting for, or what definite result can be expected. If we pummel the South ever so hard, they will love us none the better for it, and even if we subjugate them, our next step should be to cut them adrift." He never viewed the war as a great humanitarian effort to wipe out slavery. He saw it as the inevitable outcome of two incompatible systems of living. North and South. "We never were one people," he said, "and never really had a country since the Constitution was formed."

Julian, who could hardly wait till he was old enough to enlist, began drilling with his schoolmates. "If I were young enough," said his father, "I would volunteer, but as the case stands, I shall keep quiet till the enemy gets within a mile of my house."

In the first years, the war went badly for Lincoln's army. Defeat after defeat disheartened the North. Hawthorne was one of those who thought it better to let the South go, ending the bloodshed, than to see the Union returned to what it was.

As the casualties on the battlefronts mounted, young men he knew were added to them. Lowell's nephew was killed, and Oliver Wendell Holmes's son was wounded. Hawthorne's response was sardonic if not callous: "Who cares what the war costs in blood or treasure? People must die, whether a bullet kills them or no; and money must be spent, if not for gunpowder, then for worse luxuries."

During the war years, he tried hard to get on with his writing. Day after day he sat at his desk in the tower room. He thought he would have another romance ready for the public very soon. But he could not bring any of his efforts to their right ending. His stories centered on the theme he could not give up—the loss of Eden, the fall from grace, the cost of sin.

On the margins of his unfinished manuscripts are sad comments on how poorly he was doing. Sophia was painfully aware of how despondent he had become. Writing to Ticknor she said he was "low in tone and spirits. . . . he has lost the zest for life."

In painful contrast to Hawthorne's failure to produce was the example of the British novelist Anthony Trollope, whose work

Hawthorne admired. The two met when Fields gave a dinner for the visiting writer and had Hawthorne and other authors as guests. Bragging to them at table, Trollope said he worked like a cobbler making shoes whose only care is to make honest stitches. Day after day, he was up at five and always writing a specified number of pages before breakfast.

For months Hawthorne's friend Thoreau had been rapidly sinking because of an advanced stage of tuberculosis. With the little energy left him he edited his unpublished manuscripts in the hope they would bring some income to his mother and sister. Then, on May 6, 1862, the end came. Thoreau was only forty-four.

At the funeral services, Emerson read the eulogy. Hawthorne and Sophia stood among the mourners at the burial ground. Hawthorne meant to write a tribute to his friend, but it was another of his failed efforts. A year later, he told Fields, "How Thoreau would scorn me for thinking that *I* could perpetuate *him*! And I don't think so."

Portrait of President Lincoln

In March 1862, as the guest of Horatio Bridge, Hawthorne spent a few weeks traveling to Washington and the war-torn area around the capital. He prepared a journalistic report on his observations for the *Atlantic Monthly* (now edited by Fields) of July 1862. As part of a Massachusetts delegation he visited President Lincoln in the White House. His description of the president, omitted from the piece at Fields' request, gives us what Mark Van Doren called "one of the best sketches of Lincoln ever drawn":

By and by there was a little stir on the staircase and in the passageway, and in lunged a tall, loose-jointed figure, of an exaggerated Yankee port and demeanor, whom (as being about the homeliest man I ever saw, yet by no means repulsive or disagreeable) it was impossible not to recognize as Uncle Abe. Unquestionably, Western man though he be, and Kentuckian by birth, President Lincoln is the essential representative of all Yankees, and the veritable specimen, physically, of what the world seems determined to regard as our characteristic qualities. It is the strangest and yet the fitting thing in the jumble of human vicissitudes that he, out of so many millions, unlooked for, unselected by an intelligible process that could be based upon his genuine qualities, unknown to those who chose him, and unsuspected of what endowments may adapt him for his tremendous responsibility, should have found the way open for him to fling his lank personality into the chair of state, where, I presume, it was his first impulse to throw his legs on the council table and tell the Cabinet Ministers a story. There is no describing his lengthy awkwardness nor the uncouthness of his

movement; and yet it seemed as if I had been in the habit of seeing him daily, and had shaken hands with him a thousand times
in some village street; so true was he to the aspect of the pattern
American, though with a certain extravagance which, possibly, I
exaggerated still further by the delighted eagerness with which I
took it in. If put to guess his calling and livelihood, I should have
taken him for a country schoolmaster as soon as anything else.
He was dressed in a rusty black frock coat and pantaloons,
unbrushed, and worn so faithfully that the suit had adapted itself
to the curves and angularities of his figure, and had grown to be

an outer skin of the man. He had shabby slippers on his feet. His hair was black, still unmixed with gray, still, somewhat bushy, and had apparently been acquainted with neither brush nor comb that morning, after the disarrangement of the pillow; and as to a nightcap, Uncle Abe probably knows nothing of such effeminacies. His complexion is dark and sallow, betokening, I fear, an insalubrious atmosphere around the White House; he has thick black eyebrows and an impending brow, his nose is large, and the lines about his mouth are very strongly defined. The whole physiognomy is as coarse a one as you would meet anywhere in the length and breadth of the States; but withal, it is redeemed, illuminated, softened, and brightened by a kindly though serious look out of his eyes, and an expression of homely sagacity, that seems weighted with rich results of village experience. A great deal of native sense; no bookish cultivation, no refinement; honest at heart, and thoroughly so, and yet, in some sort, sly—at least, endowed with a sort of tact and wisdom that are akin to craft, and would impel him, I think, to take an antagonist in flank, rather than to make a bull-run at him right in front. But, on the whole, I like this sallow, queer, sagacious visage, with the homely human sympathies that warmed it; and, for my small share in the matter, would as lief have Uncle Abe for a ruler as any man whom it would have been practicable to put in his place. Immediately on his entrance the President accosted our member of Congress, who had us in charge, and, with a comical twist of his face, made some jocular remark about the length of his breakfast. He then greeted us all round, not waiting for an introduction, but shaking and squeezing everybody's hand with the utmost cordiality, whether the individual's name was announced to him or not. His manner towards us was wholly without pretense, but yet had a kind of natural dignity, quite sufficient to keep the forwardest of us from clapping him on the shoulder and asking him for a story.

Asleep, Forever

THERE WAS ONE MORE—the last—book to be published, in 1863. It was *Our Old Home*, adapted from Hawthorne's journals during the years he spent in England. Against Fields' urging, he insisted on dedicating the book to Pierce, who had recently attacked President Lincoln for issuing the Emancipation Proclamation freeing slaves without constitutional authority. Hawthorne said, "I cannot, merely on account of pecuniary profit or literary reputation, go back from what I have deliberately felt and thought it right to do; and if I were to tear out the dedication, I should never look at the volume again without remorse and shame."

The book proved a mild success, with about 6,500 copies sold. American readers and critics enjoyed it especially because of Hawthorne's humorous thrusts at the way the English lived. English readers, however, were angered by what they took to be abuse from a man who had enjoyed their hospitality and then turned on them.

The book appeared right after the terrible July riots in New York when mobs took to the streets protesting against a conscription law that let rich men avoid army service by payment of $300 or by procuring a substitute to enlist for three years. Burning down the draft office, they then shifted their anger to the blacks and abolitionists. Three days of shooting, burning, looting, and lynching ensued, until ten thousand federal troops finally stopped the violence. More than a thousand people were killed or injured.

Early in December, when Pierce's wife Jane died, Hawthorne, though weakened by illness, journeyed to New Hampshire for the funeral. He was worse upon his return home, with a stomach disorder, fainting spells, and nosebleeds. And so feeble he could neither read nor write. Installments of romances he struggled to write appeared in several issues of the *Atlantic Monthly* in 1860 through 1863, but he told Fields he was sure he would never finish them.

But his family found him hard to take. He was so depressed, so irritable, impossible to talk with, and sunk deep within himself.

Sophia wrote their friend Bridge that she felt "the wildest anxiety about him, because he has wasted away very much, and the suns in his eyes are collapsed, and he has had no spirits, no appetite, and very little sleep . . . The state of our country has, doubtless, excessively depressed him."

Hearing of his sickness, Franklin Pierce came to Concord for a visit. Maybe a trip into the springtime countryside of New Hampshire would be helpful, he suggested. On May 12, 1864, the two old friends set out in Pierce's private carriage. A few days later, Pierce saw that Hawthorne's condition was worsening. He walked with difficulty, his mind seemed blurred. Pierce wanted him to stop for a while at a hotel to rest. But Hawthorne insisted they go on.

Nathaniel Hawthorne died peacefully in this hotel in Plymouth, New Hampshire, on May 19, 1864.

That night they took two adjoining rooms in a hotel in Plymouth, New Hampshire. Hawthorne went to bed in his room at nine. At one, Pierce looked in on him; he was sleeping on his side. Two hours later he checked him again. And found that he had died in his sleep. It was May 19, 1864. Hawthorne was fifty-nine years old.

His body was returned to Concord on May 21. He was buried on the afternoon of May 23 in Concord's Sleepy Hollow Cemetery. Present with his family were Fields, Emerson, Longfellow, Alcott, Whittier, Lowell, Holmes—and Pierce. In his journal, Emerson wrote, "Yesterday, May 23, we buried Hawthorne in Sleepy Hollow... I thought there was a tragic element in the event—in the painful solitude of the man, which, I suppose, could no longer be endured, and he died of it."

It is not know what the precise cause of death was. It may have been cancer of some internal organ, for everyone had noticed that he had seemed to be wasting away.

* * *

Emerson's sad comment on Hawthorne echoed what Hawthorne himself set down in his journal. On January 1, 1864, some five months before he would die, he wrote, "I have fallen into a quagmire of disgust and despondency with respect to literary matters. I am tired of my own thoughts and fancies, and my own mode of expressing them." He was looking back on the last six years when he had struggled to write four novels, failing to finish any of them.

Yet in his own lifetime, his work earned the respect and admiration of such writers as Edgar Allan Poe and Herman Melville. And today, almost 150 years since his passing, he is valued as one of America's great writers of fiction.

Within Sleepy Hollow Cemetery in Concord, Massachusetts, there is an elevated section known as Author's Ridge. Nathaniel Hawthorne's grave is there as are those of his friends Henry David Thoreau and Ralph Waldo Emerson.

Life After Hawthorne

The family continued to live at the Wayside four more years after Hawthorne's death. When the cost of living rose and the income from his books shrank, they moved for a while to Dresden, Germany, because it was cheaper. Then, with the children off on their own, Sophia moved to London, where she still had friends. She died there of typhoid pneumonia in 1871 and was buried at Kensal Green, thousands of miles from Hawthorne's grave.

The children went different ways. Una became engaged to a young poet who soon died of tuberculosis. She lived off and on with her sister or brother and then in an Anglican convent. Often ill, on the verge of mental breakdown, she died at the age of thirty-three. Julian took to writing, capitalizing on his father's name, and pouring out novels, histories, essays, and a biography of his parents. He married young and had ten children. In 1913, at age sixty-six, he served a brief term in prison for selling shares in a worthless mine. He died in 1934.

Rose, the youngest, was married at twenty to a writer who was an alcoholic. She lost her only child to diphtheria, and divorced. She converted to Catholicism and, as a self-ordained Sister of Mercy, dedicated her life to caring for the poor and the sick. As Sister Rose, she launched one of the first hospices in America, on the Lower East Side of New York City. Later she established the Rosary Hill Home for indigent patients with incurable cancer. It still functions in Hawthorne, New York. She died in 1926.

A Note on Sources

A biographer of Nathaniel Hawthorne has a rich treasury of sources to draw upon. First of all are Hawthorne's own writings— his novels and stories, of course, but also his journals, his letters, and the letters of family, friends, and others who corresponded with him. Many people who figured in his life at one time or another recorded their impressions of him. And then there are the references to him in the public documents where he lived and worked.

So what is the biographer to do with an immense amount of material? His choice of what to use is determined by his own values. Any biography is influenced by its author's point of view. That is why there can be several biographies of the same person, each different to varying degree from the others.

All the quotations found in this book were taken from what Hawthorne or others said or wrote. These are all documented in the sources I used—his own works and those listed in the selected bibliography.

Source Notes

12–14 Edwin Haviland Miller, *Salem Is My Dwelling Place: A Life of Nathaniel Hawthorne* (Iowa City: University of Iowa Press, 1991), p. 21.

19 Miller, p. 14.

19 Ibid.

19 Ibid., p. 15.

19 Margaret B. Moore, *The Salem World of Nathaniel Hawthorne* (Columbia: University of Missouri Press, 1998), p. 27.

22 Miller, p. 30.

24 Moore, p. 89.

24–25 Ibid.

25 Ibid., p. 91.

25 Ibid., p. 93.

26 (Miller, p. 55.

27 James McIntosh, *Nathaniel Hawthorne's Tales* (New York: Norton, 1987), p. 295.

27 Ibid., p. 295.

31 James R. Mellow, *Nathaniel Hawthorne in His Times* (Baltimore: Johns Hopkins University Press, 1998), p. 34.

34 Van Wyck Brooks, *The Flowering of New England, 1815–1865* (New York: Dutton, 1936), p. 223.

34 Ibid., p. 275.

34 Miller, p. 89.

36 Ibid., p. 89.

36 Mark Van Doren, *Nathaniel Hawthorne* (New York: Viking, 1949), p. 26.

36 Mellow, p. 44.

37 Ibid., p. 58.

42 Miller, p. 101.

42–43 McIntosh, p. 296.

43 Ibid., p. 298.

44 Van Doren, p. 62.

46 Ibid.

48 Miller, p. 126.

48 Ibid., p. 132.

49 Ibid., p. 144.

49 Ibid.

49 Ibid., p. 164.

51 Miller, p. 150.

51 Ibid., p. 166.

52 Mellow, p. 164.

53 Nathaniel Hawthorne, *Liberty Tree: With the Last Words of Grandfather's Chair* (Boston: E. P. Peabody, 1841)

53 Mellow, p. 194.

55 Ibid., p. 161.

55 Ibid.

56 Ibid.

56 Van Doren, p. 100.

56 Ibid.

56 Mellow, p. 162.

56 Miller, p. 170.

56–57 Mellow, p. 163.

57–58 Van Doren, p. 103.

58 Sean Manley, *Nathaniel Hawthorne: Captain of the Imagination* (New York: Vanguard, 1968), p. 89.

60 Miller, p. 170.

61 Mellow, p. 178.

62 Randall Stewart, *Nathaniel Hawthorne* (New Haven: Yale University Press, 1948), p. 59.

63 Ibid.

63–65 Miller, pp. 182–199.

66 Ibid., p. 216.

67 Ibid., p. 217.

68 Ibid.

69 Ibid.

70 Ibid., p. 216.

70 Ibid., p. 227.

70–71 Ibid., p. 217.

71–72 Mellow, p. 217.

72 Brenda Wineapple, *Hawthorne: A Life* (New York: Knopf, 2003), p. 112.

73 Ibid.

73 Mellow, p. 227.

73 Ibid.

73–74 Ibid.

74 Ibid.

76 Ibid., p. 234.

78 Stewart, p. 69.

78 Ibid.

78 Ibid., p. 71.

79 Ibid., p. 72.

79 Ibid. p. 73.

86 Ibid. p. 82.

86–87 Ibid., p. 83.

87 Ibid.

87 Ibid.

89 Miller, p. 280.

90 Van Doren, p. 141.

91 Ibid.

94 Robert Cantwell, *Nathaniel Hawthorne: The American Years* (New York: Rinehart, 1948), p. 438.

95 Mellow, p. 315.

95 Ibid.

95 Ibid.

95 Ibid.

97 Miller, p. 310.

98 Ibid., p. 314.

98–99 Stewart, p. 70.

99 Miller, p. 316.

100 Nathaniel Hawthorne, *The House of Seven Gables* (New York: Barnes & Noble, 2000), p. 9.

101 Van Doren, p. 172.

101 Ibid.

101 Ibid., p. 142.

101 Ibid., p. 170.

101–102 Miller, p. 345.

102 Ibid.

102 Ibid., p. 388.

103 Mellow, p. 392.

104 Ibid.

104 Miller, p. 381.

105 Ibid.

107 Ibid.

108 Ibid., p. 149.

108 Ibid., p. 149.

109 Stewart, p. 133.

109 Ibid.

109 Mellow, p. 410

110 Milton Meltzer and Walter Harding, *A Thoreau Profile* (New York: Thomas Y. Crowell, 1962), p. 200.

111 Ibid., p. 205.

112 Mellow, p. 421.

114 Miller, p. 399.

114 Ibid., p. 400.

114 Ibid.

115 Ibid., p. 402.

115 Ibid.

116 Ibid., p. 449.

116 Van Doren, p. 145.

117 Ibid., p. 452.

117–118 Ibid., p. 461.

118 Van Doren, p. 208.

119 Mellow, p. 472.

119–120 Miller, p. 478.

120 Wineapple, p. 282.

120 Ibid.

120 Ibid.

121 Van Doren, p. 219.

122 Van Wyck Brooks, p. 469.

123–124 Stewart, p. 190.

124–125 bid., p. 208.

125–126 Ibid., pp. 192–93.

126 Ibid.

126 Van Doren, p. 220.

129 Miller, p. 445.

130 Wineapple, p. 224.

130 Ibid., p. 326.

130 Ibid.

130 Miller, p. 444.

131 Ibid.

132 Moore, p. 244.

132–133 Mellow, p. 536.

133 Miller, p. 442.

133–134 Wineapple, p. 334.

134 Mellow, p. 541.

134 Ibid., p. 542.

135 Ibid., p. 544.

135 Miller, p. 467.

135 Mellow, p. 559.

136 Van Doren, p. 225.

137 Ibid.

137–139 Milton Meltzer, *Voices from the Civil War* (New York: Thomas Y. Crowell, 1989), pp. 27–30.

140 Miller, p. 502.

141 Mellow, p. 574.

142–143 Van Doren, p. 265.

143 Miller, p. 505.

Selected Bibliography

Brooks, Van Wyck. *The Flowering of New England, 1815–1865.* New York: Dutton, 1936.

Cantwell, Robert. *Nathaniel Hawthorne: The American Years.* New York: Rinehart, 1948.

James, Henry. *Hawthorne.* Ithaca, NY: Cornell University Press, 1997.

Manley, Sean. *Nathaniel Hawthorne: Captain of the Imagination.* New York: Vanguard, 1968.

Mellow, James R. *Nathaniel Hawthorne in His Times.* Baltimore: Johns Hopkins University Press, 1998.

Miller, Edwin Haviland. *Salem Is My Dwelling Place: A Life of Nathaniel Hawthorne.* Iowa City: University of Iowa Press, 1991.

Moore, Margaret B. *The Salem World of Nathaniel Hawthorne.* Columbia: University of Missouri Press, 1998.

Myerson, Joel, ed. *Selected Letters of Nathaniel Hawthorne.* Columbus: Ohio State University Press. 2002.

Normand, Jean. *Nathaniel Hawthorne: An Approach to the Analysis of Artistic Creation.* Cleveland: Case Western Reserve University Press, 1970.

150   Rusk, Ralph L. *The Life of Ralph Waldo Emerson*. New York: Scribner's, 1949.

Steele, Jeffrey, ed. *The Essential Margaret Fuller*. New Brunswick, NJ: Rutgers University Press, 1992.

Stewart, Randall. *Nathaniel Hawthorne*. New Haven, CT: Yale University Press, 1948.

Van Doren, Mark. *Nathaniel Hawthorne*. New York: Viking, 1949.

Wineapple, Brenda. *Hawthorne: A Life*. New York: Knopf, 2003.

Reading Hawthorne Himself

Many of Hawthorne's tales and novels are available in inexpensive editions. The following is a list of those I made use of:

The House of the Seven Gables. New York: Barnes & Noble, 2000.

The Marble Faun. New York: Penguin, 1990.

Nathaniel Hawthorne's Tales. New York: W. W. Norton, 1987.

The Scarlet Letter. New York: Barnes & Noble, 2003.

Tanglewood Tales for Girls and Boys. New York: Tor, 1999.

Twenty Days with Julian & Little Bunny by Papa. New York: NYRB Books, 2003.

The Whole History of Grandfather's Chair or True Stories from New England History 1620–1808. McLean, VA: Indy, n.d.

A Wonder Book for Girls and Boys. New York: Tor, 1998.

Hawthorne Websites

Hawthorne Community Association
   http://www.pivot.net/~hawthorne/
   This website has information about the Hawthorne house near
   Sebago Lake, Maine, where Hawthorne spent his adolescence.

Hawthorne in Salem
   http://www.hawthorneinsalem.org/Introduction.html
   This website is rich with information on Hawthorne's life, family,
   and writings, as well as houses in Salem. Includes links to full-text
   versions of Hawthorne's literature.

The House of the Seven Gables
   http://www.7gables.org/
   Find information at this website on the mysterious Salem
   mansion on which Hawthorne based his novel by the same
   name. His boyhood home also now sits on this historic site.

The Old Manse National Historic Site
   http://www.concord.org/town/manse/old_manse.html
   This website offers information on the historic property where
   Nathaniel and Sophia spent their first three years of marriage, and
   where Ralph Waldo Emerson spent parts of his childhood.

Peabody Essex Museum
   http://www.pem.org/homepage/
   This website takes you to the Phillips Library of this museum,
   which contains numerous original Hawthorne manuscripts,
   literary criticisms, and all the American editions of his works. This
   feature also includes images of various Hawthorne personal items
   and other writings.

Chronology of Nathaniel Hawthorne

1804	Born July 4 in Salem.
1811	Suffers lameness from foot injury.
1816–19	With his two sisters and mother, lives on Manning Property at Raymond, Maine.
1819–21	Returns to Salem for college preparatory studies.
1821–25	Attends Bowdoin College in Brunswick, Maine. Classmates include Henry Wadsworth Longfellow and Franklin Pierce.
1825–39	Lives in Salem in mother's house. Takes occasional short trips. Wide reading, intensive study of New England history. Develops skills as writer.
1828	Publishes *Fanshawe* anonymously, at own expense.
1830–39	Later, attempts to destroy all copies. Dozens of stories appear anonymously in magazines and newspapers.
1836	Lives in Boston, editing and writing for *American Magazine of Useful and Entertaining Knowledge*.

1837	*Twice-Told Tales* published. First important work. Engaged to Sophia Peabody of Salem.
1839–40	Inspector to Boston Custom House. *Grandfather's Chair,* history of New England, for children.
1841	Lives at Brook Farm community in West Roxbury, Massachusetts. Leaves after eight months.
1842	Second edition of *Twice-Told Tales,* in two volumes. On July 9, marries Sophia Peabody. They move to Concord, Massachusetts, and rent the Old Manse.
1842–45	Writes and publishes variety of tales and sketches.
1844	Daughter Una born.
1845	Edits Horatio Bridge's *Journal of an African Cruiser.*
1846	Publishes *Mosses from an Old Manse.* Son Julian born.
1846–49	Surveyor in Salem Custom House.
1850	Publishes *The Scarlet Letter.* Moves to Lenox in western Massachusetts. Becomes friend of Herman Melville.
1851	Publishes *The House of the Seven Gables, The Snow-Image and Other Twice-Told Tales,* and *The Wonder Book,* children's stories. Last child, Rose, born.
1852	Returns to Concord to live in the Wayside, formerly the Alcott home. Writes *The Life of Franklin Pierce,* a campaign biography for friend who wins the presidency. Publishes *The Blithedale Romance.*
1853	Publishes *Tanglewood Tales for Girls and Boys.* Appointed U.S. consul at Liverpool, England, by President Pierce. Serves to 1857.
1858–59	Lives in Rome and Florence, Italy.

1859–60	Returns to England.
1860	Publishes *The Marble Faun*, his last novel. Returns to the Wayside in Concord. Health begins to deteriorate.
1862–63	Travels to Washington and Virginia battlegrounds. His report published in the *Atlantic Monthly*.
1863	Publishes *Our Old Home*, a book of essays on his experience in England, his last publication during his lifetime. Continues work on several novels; fragments published after his death.
1864	Leaves home for last journey with friend Pierce and dies in Plymouth, New Hampshire, on May 19. Buried in Sleepy Hollow Cemetery, Concord, on May 23.

Index

Page numbers in *italics* refer to illustrations.

About the Author

The life of Nathaniel Hawthorne is the latest in Meltzer's series of biographies of writers. These include Mark Twain, Lydia Maria Child, Langston Hughes, Walt Whitman, Carl Sandburg, Edgar Allan Poe, Herman Melville, and Emily Dickinson.

In 2001 Meltzer received the Laura Ingalls Wilder Award from the American Library Association for his "substantial and lasting contributions to literature for children." The year before, the Catholic Library Association awarded him the Regina Medal for lifetime achievement. Five of his books have been finalists for the National Book Award. He has won the Carter G. Woodson, Christopher, Jane Addams, Jefferson Cup, Olive Branch, and Golden Kite awards. His titles frequently appear in the "best books of the year" lists of the American Library Association, the National Council for the Social Studies, the National Council of Teachers of English, and the New York Times Best Books of the Year lists.

Born in Worcester, Massachusetts, Meltzer was educated at Columbia University. He lives with his wife in New York City. They have two daughters and two grandsons.